BEATING STRESS
IN THE NHS

Ruth Chambers
Anthony Schwartz
and
Elizabeth Boath

Radcliffe Medical Press

Radcliffe Medical Press Ltd
18 Marcham Road
Abingdon
Oxon OX14 1AA
United Kingdom

www.radcliffe-oxford.com
The Radcliffe Medical Press electronic catalogue and online ordering facility.
Direct sales to anywhere in the world.

_____

© 2003 Ruth Chambers, Anthony Schwartz and Elizabeth Boath

Cartoons © 2003 Martin Davies

British Library Cataloguing in Publication Data

A catalogue record for this book is available from the British Library.

ISBN 1 85775 927 3

Typeset by Advance Typesetting Ltd, Oxfordshire
Printed and bound by TJ International Ltd, Padstow, Cornwall

Contents

About the authors

Ruth Chambers has been a GP for 20 years. Her previous experience has encompassed a wide range of research and educational activities, including stress and the health of doctors, the quality of healthcare, healthy working and many other topics.

She is currently a part-time GP and the Professor of Primary Care Development at the School of Health, Staffordshire University. Her doctorate was based on the health and well-being of doctors. Ruth set up a local support scheme for doctors in 1994 and has since run it with the help of other GPs, psychologists, psychiatrists and counsellors. Much of her work over the last ten years has focused on urging GPs and others to improve doctors' conditions both at work and in their home lives. Ruth has initiated and run many different types of educational initiatives and activities in relation to doctors' stress and ill health.

Anthony Schwartz, as a Doctor of Psychology, is a Member of the British Psychological Society and a chartered clinical and health psychologist who specialises in personal and professional development. He is director of Arcadia Alive, Consultancy, Training and Development, which specialises in the 'human factors' at work, and runs various organisational programmes to enhance the ability of managers and staff to cope with change and to manage people, pressure and performance. The focus of his professional work in the NHS is in physical health, where he works part-time as a consultant clinical psychologist. He also runs a clinical psychology practice, and is a tutor on the doctoral programme in clinical psychology at the University of Birmingham and a fellow at the Centre for Health Policy and Practice at Staffordshire University. He has over 15 years' experience in psychology, working across the disciplines of nursing, medicine, physical and mental health. This has been predominantly within the NHS, dealing with staff stress and performance, and with supervision and facilitation in areas where people work under challenging conditions. Increasingly, he has been working in the field of 'health at work', linking with professionals in occupational health and human resources to implement practical strategies to empower people in organisations, through interactive and experiential learning. His academic activities include conducting research, making regular conference presentations, running workshops, involvement in ongoing personal development training (e.g. coaching, supervision and mentoring) and facilitating learning forums.

Elizabeth Boath is Head of the Centre for Health Policy and Practice at Staffordshire University. She has a keen interest in mental health, particularly perinatal mental health, and this is reflected by her extensive publications in this area. She is a member of the West Midlands Primary Mental Health Network. She has a degree in psychology, and her PhD addressed the cost-effectiveness of two alternative approaches to the treatment of postnatal depression. She has been involved in health services research for over 14 years as a researcher, research facilitator and lecturer, and she has taught on a wide range of topics, including critical appraisal skills, evidence-based practice, clinical governance and clinical effectiveness.

Introduction: using this book to beat stress at work

This is not a comprehensive book on stress management. What it does offer is a wide selection of ideas and approaches to help *you* beat stress at work in the NHS (or should we say stress *from* working in the NHS)?

This book is intended for anyone working in the health service, whether you are a health professional, a manager or a member of the support staff, at any level of seniority and in any healthcare setting. No one is immune from stress, and some people create stress *for* others.

The aim of this book is to provide you with opportunities and options to control and minimise stress that arises from your work in the health service. It should help you to maintain a sense of balance amidst the change and turmoil of successive NHS reorganisations, and to become more resilient to stress.

There are interactive exercises throughout to give you an opportunity to assess your learning needs and to reflect on how the ideas about which you have just read apply to you and your circumstances. You should transfer information from these exercises to your own personal development plan.

Chapter 1 sets the scene. You will realise that the way in which the NHS is run generates stress for members of the workforce every day. You can learn how to control stress that arises from patients' demands, excessive workload, multiple reorganisations of the health service and the plethora of Government directives. We shall remind you that you cannot control stress by yourself – you need to work with colleagues to minimise the sources of stress and deal with the effects of stress on you all.

Chapter 2 focuses on why, when and how stress occurs in the workplace in the health service. If you know and understand how stress originates, it is more likely that you will recognise its adverse effects in your workplace, in yourself and in colleagues – and take appropriate action.

Chapter 3 offers an Aladdin's cave of methods to reduce or control stress as an individual. You can use these by yourself to reduce the sources of stress or to combat the effects of stress on you. Alternatively, you and colleagues can discuss the various techniques as a form of 'self-help' group. This is a long chapter, and it may take you a year or more to try out the different ideas and challenges described within it – to experiment and find the methods that suit you best.

In Chapter 4 you are encouraged to think of what the team can do to control stress for individual team members, through organisational means. This will not stem the flow of stresses and pressures from the wider NHS, but it will encourage you to think of what control is within your power. Harness clinical governance as a vehicle to improve organisational systems and procedures so that there is less stress and pressure for you and your team in your practice or workplace.

It is important to incorporate stress management into your framework of lifelong learning and revitalise yourself. Chapter 5 contains ideas for your self-development that involve focusing your personal development plan on stress management.

Do you ever wonder why, despite your good resolutions, nothing much seems to change? You do well at first in keeping up your good intentions, but then something crops up to undermine your resolutions, and you resume your bad old ways. Well, the final chapter will guide you to approach the challenge of minimising stress in your life as a 'project'. You are introduced to the logical framework approach and encouraged to think out your action plan in a truly logical way, as well as realise the assumptions you are making in setting out the stages of your plan, and the potential risks of things going wrong. You could also use the same logical framework approach for other action plans on different topics in the future.

Having worked through this book and the associated exercises, you will be able to make changes to your working life both as an individual and as a team in your practice or workplace.

Not all pressure is harmful. A certain amount of pressure can enhance your performance and help to bring colleagues together for a common purpose – for example, to develop new work or to meet a challenge. However, excessive unrelenting negative pressure results in individuals experiencing stress to a greater or lesser extent, depending on how resilient they are and what other factors are changing in their lives.

You will derive additional benefits from reading and working through this book if you pass on to your patients much of what you learn.

1

Beating stress at work in the NHS: setting the scene

Thirty years ago people expected 'a job for life', and had a clearer idea of what life held in store for them. The pace of life was slower and people knew how to respond in most situations. Today, life has changed. The organisation that people work for may not exist in two years' time, or it may fall foul of a 'reorganisation'. Organisations and society have become unsympathetic to 'fallen people'. As a result of this competitive environment we have lost a sense of security (even if it might have been a false one). Although we have much more wealth than previous generations, we are more focused on anxiety and we experience much guilt.

The concept of those working in the healthcare professions as 'being here to serve' is admirable – but not at the expense of the health needs of the staff doing the 'serving'. The cliché that 'people are our most valuable assets' has seldom been reflected as action by the NHS supporting healthcare workers. Plenty of research studies have revealed that working in the health service is bad for your health!

Box 1.1:   Retirement from ill health in the NHS workforce

The relative rates of retirement on ill health grounds reflect how well the various disciplines within the NHS workforce are faring at work. The overall rate of retirement because of ill health in the NHS was 5.5 per 1000 employees in England and Wales in 1998–99.[1]

Ambulance workers had the highest rates of ill health retirement, with 15 out of 1000 retiring that year, compared with nurses (5 out of 1000), doctors (5 out of 1000) and healthcare assistants or support staff (13 out of 1000).[1] Two-thirds of these ambulance workers and half of the nurses retired because of musculoskeletal disease problems, compared with a quarter of doctors who retired because of ill health. One-third of doctors, one-fifth of nurses, one-tenth of healthcare assistants or support staff and one-sixth of ambulance workers who retired on the grounds of ill health did so for psychiatric reasons.

Although the NHS has a clear focus on improving services, the role of the healthcare professional and their needs (e.g. for support, learning and affirmation) cannot be ignored if national policies are to succeed. Surveys of those working for the NHS continue to show that there is widespread dis-heartenment and low morale. Change will always be around. Your challenge as a health professional is to see change as an opportunity to develop and grow both as a person and as a professional, and to seek out and develop self-management and support structures to enable you to work more happily.

Reasons for nurses leaving the NHS

An interview study of ex-nurses who had left the NHS found that a variety of reasons were given to explain why they had left, including the following:[2]

- lack of career progression
- limited professional development
- resistance to service improvements
- non-family-friendly working patterns
- bullying, inflexible and hierarchical management
- poor morale
- dangerous or inadequate staff–patient ratios
- increased patient activity resulting in poorer care because of overload
- lack of resources to meet identified needs
- a 'make-do' culture
- poor working conditions
- pay not commensurate with responsibility and autonomy
- excessive case loads
- difficulty in influencing decisions
- quality of care ignored
- poor team spirit.

How the NHS should value staff

The extracts quoted in Box 1.2 opposite highlight the far-ranging review and action that the NHS needs to take on if it is to retain staff. We need to convert the working environment into one where far fewer trained staff leave their professions after just a few years of working in unacceptable, stress-provoking conditions.

Box 1.2:   Value trained staff in the NHS workforce

'The UK and many other countries need to enhance, reorientate and integrate their workforce planning capacity across occupations and disciplines to identify the skills and roles needed to meet identified service needs. They can also improve the day-to-day matching of nurse (and other NHS workforce) staffing with workload. Flexibility should be about using working patterns that are efficient, but which also support nurses (and others in the NHS workforce) in maintaining a balance between their work and personal life.'[3]

'A wider perspective is needed to achieve clarity of roles and a better balance of registered nurses, physicians, other health professionals and support workers. The evidence to support various types of skill mix is developing ... Why have these wider-reaching interventions not been more systematically implemented? The very fact that they have a wider reach means that they often challenge current practice, health systems inertia and vested interests.'[4]

There have been many calls for preventative training, counselling and stress management services, since high costs are incurred if well-trained personnel are lost to the service.[4,5] The loss of a doctor, nurse or other health professional incurs training and replacement costs, as well as all kinds of tangible and intangible costs arising from the organisational disruption that this causes. The costs of ill health to the health service are high – in terms of the days lost due to absence, the expense of training or retraining staff, and the knock-on effects on morale.

Box 1.3:   Survey of hospital consultants has shown a drop in morale[6]

A survey of more than 1500 consultants who treat emergency patients found that more than half of those surveyed said that their job satisfaction was poor (17%) or moderate (39%). The three most pressing concerns were as follows:

*   increasing intensity of work
*   not enough trainees or trainee hours
*   decreasing quality or lack of continuity of patient care.

What the Government and health service organisations can do

The way that we work in the health service is directly influenced by the plethora of initiatives and directives from the Government, health bodies, professional groups and consumer associations, which create national and local imperatives. The details and implications of these initiatives and directives are poorly

communicated to the workforce as a whole, who in turn find it difficult to
cope with the change and uncertainty. We need to develop a positive concept
of work in a supportive working environment, where we enjoy our work and
are not there just in order to earn enough money to live.

Occupational healthcare services for the one million or so members of the
NHS workforce are patchy and only readily available to a minority of workers.
In the past, many employers within the NHS have viewed inability to cope
with stress as a failing of the employee, for which the individual concerned
should be responsible. They have not recognised that organisational pressures
have contributed to that employee suffering from stress and that, as employers,
they have organisational and corporate responsibilities. The employer has a
legal duty to take an interest in the causes of stress and primary prevention,
as well as treatment and rehabilitation of any of their employees who suffer
ill health arising from work-related stress. Stress is multifactorial in terms of
causes and outcomes. The management of systems and processes within the
practice, trust or primary care organisation is key to preventing or reducing
stress and pressures for their employees. The performance of an individual is
affected both by the person him- or herself and the environment. This is illus-
trated by the equation $B = P + E$, which indicates that a person's behaviour
(B) is a function of that person and the environment (E). We need to focus on
both – the individual and the environment – when examining stress.

Quality assurance

Quality assurance has brought with it an increased emphasis on accountability
and demands on professionals to show service improvements and clinical
effectiveness. As a result, health professionals and managers are experiencing
an increased sense of pressure to perform. Patients' demands and expectations
continue to rise, too. Such added pressures have affected the morale and
enthusiasm of those working in healthcare, despite the fact that most staff
affirm the benefits of many of the changes to the NHS and patient care in
general. Clinical governance and continuing professional development are
two approaches which are central to today's health service culture that
can help you to control stress as an individual or workplace team through
personal and organisational change.

The NHS has a framework that focuses on a number of areas for improving
patient services and care. This includes renewal and change in:

* developing, setting and monitoring standards of healthcare
* partnership working with other agencies (e.g. local authorities)
* integration of health and social services (e.g. care trusts)
* cost-effective and efficient services
* quality of care.

Look after yourself

As a health professional you should be proactive in maintaining good health maintenance strategies for yourself as well as for the population as a whole. You will not thrive at work if you are under undue stress for too long a period of time. Studies of health at work in the NHS show that unhealthy stress is related to the following:

• high workload and pressure of work
• lack of role clarity, and role conflict
• long hours and lack of control over work
• poor management style and poor interrelationships at work
• poor social support at work
• conflict between demands of work and family.

You need to learn to minimise the stresses on you and your colleagues that are caused by the pressures of achieving changes to patient services and care. There is only so much that you can do yourself – the organisation that you work for has a responsibility to look after your interests, too. When NHS managers are planning to develop, set and monitor standards, they should consider the impact on staff and neutralise the additional work that results through more resources, more skills, more efficient processes and systems, etc. Co-ordinating work with other agencies should reduce duplication of effort and decrease the overall workload for both sets of staff. The improved quality of patient care should not be at the staff's expense through the introduction of 'family-unfriendly' working hours, for example, or a disproportionate weighting of patients' views leading to NHS systems that are unfair to staff's welfare.

Box 1.4

I can't keep up with all the changes. You come to work one week, you're ex-pected to do things one way, and then a few weeks later you are told that it's not done that way any more. Sometimes I think changes are made just for the sake of it.

(Practice nurse)

Job satisfaction

Job satisfaction is really important. We know that the professional who is motivated is more likely to encourage and enthuse his or her patients and colleagues, and that reasonable levels of job satisfaction can protect a person against stress.[5,7,8] So much of the care that is given to patients in the healthcare setting is about 'human factors', in addition to the technical skills of being a practitioner.

The importance of promoting the job satisfaction of staff is increasingly acknowledged as important by managers in healthcare, and the way in which that links with the quality of services and care as a whole. In one study of 81 general practices, those with low job demands were twice as likely to have medium to high levels of job satisfaction as those with high job demands.[9] Those with a high degree of job control were almost ten times more likely to have medium to high levels of job satisfaction as those with a low degree of control over their job. Similarly, those with high levels of social support were almost ten times more likely to report medium to high levels of job satisfaction compared with those with little social support. Receptionists, practice nurses, district nurses and health visitors had lower levels of job satisfaction than doctors – probably because they had lower levels of control and/or support at work.

It seems that clinical autonomy is a more important determinant of job satisfaction for medical professionals than is managerial autonomy.[8] Increases in the volume or complexity of work will not necessarily lead to lower levels of job satisfaction if the changes are accompanied by increased opportunities for doctors and others to control the way in which their work is accomplished (e.g. by delegation or flexible working).

Expectations of a health professional

What do you expect from yourself, and what do others expect of you? You will have expectations and pressures arising from clinical governance, professional accreditation, national directives such as the National Service Frameworks, clinical excellence, annual appraisals, health improvement and quality. As well as the expectations that others have of you, there are also those that you demand of yourself. You have to contend with your own expectations, and you may drive yourself on to super-human standards in all of your diverse roles. We know from research that those who are self-critical about the standards of their own work are more likely to be stressed. They may be striving for perfection in their work, and if they do not meet the high standards that they set for their practice, they judge themselves harshly and put themselves under even more pressure.

Your internal expectations in terms of what you demand from yourself can be linked to your personal vision, the beliefs you hold, your role models, your need for success and your status. You will have other internally driven needs – for instance, to heal, to nurture and to help others in your role at work. Alongside this are the external expectations of others – for example, for you to

- As a human being

- As a professional

- As a partner or spouse

- As a parent, son or daughter

- As a friend

- As an employer

- As a line manager

- As a team member

Figure 1.1: Your expectations of your many roles.

be accessible, available, and infallible in your clinical or managerial roles, or in organising your home and social life as a parent or partner.

Sometimes it is just that you are trying to please people (colleagues, patients, your employers or your juniors) all of the time, and you set yourself impossible tasks. People with vulnerable personalities appear to be attracted to a medical career. They may have had over-protective parents, unstable childhoods, or problems in adjusting during adolescence. As a result, they may crave other people's approbation. One of the explanations for doctors' high rates of alcoholism, anxiety, depression and stress is the toxic combination of occupational stress and vulnerable personalities.

You may be the sort of person who constantly places more demands on yourself and keeps putting off gratification, believing that 'one day I will give myself a break'.

Professional development gives you an opportunity to be honest with yourself about your own abilities to do your job. Such a review may help you to see that your needs and skills are poorly matched with the particular post you are in, and give you an opportunity to gain new qualifications or make a career move.

What is stress?

Is stress bad?

Whether stress is bad for you depends on how much stress you are under, for how long it is applied, whether you feel powerless to stand up to the stress, or whether you are able to overcome it. A moderate amount of stress is necessary in order to perform well at work and function well in general, and to maintain a zest for life. Zero stress may lead to boredom, whereas too much stress over too long a period will lead to a person becoming indecisive, exhausted or burnt out.

An occasional event or task that generates very high levels of stress may not have as significant an effect on you as lesser causes of stress that occur every day. A steady relentless drip of stress-provoking situations may be just as likely to create a stressed person as a crisis event with monumental stress attached to it.

Work-related stress is the second largest category of occupational ill health in industry as a whole, the largest category being musculoskeletal disease. Stress affects the whole of today's society. It is estimated that at any one time around half a million people in the UK are suffering from work-related stress at a level that makes them ill. Around 6.5 million working days are lost in the UK per annum due to stress, depression or anxiety or a physical condition ascribed to work-related stress, each person taking an average 16 days off work each year. Up to 60% of absenteeism is thought to be due to mental or emotional problems. Around 10% of the workforce in the UK has been estimated to experience emotional and physical ill health related to occupational stress. This all costs society an estimated £3.8 billion (1995–96 prices).[10]

The rate of work-related stress, anxiety or depression is statistically significantly higher for workplaces that employ more than 50 people than for those that employ fewer than that number. Self-employed people have the lowest rates of work-related stress.[10]

About 7% of GP consultations involve patients with work-related stress.[11]

Dealing with demands and pressures – as an individual and as an organisation

The management of work-related pressures shows a clear link between the individual and the organisation, and the accompanying tensions and opportunities that may arise.

Pressure at work is the life source of an organisation that offers the individual excitement, challenge and a chance to achieve and make a difference. Given the 'buzz factor' that is needed, it is important to maintain a dynamic and enthusiastic organisational climate within which this can occur. Some people can get 'addicted' to such pressure or stress – and find it difficult to complete work unless they are striving to meet deadlines. You need to find a level of stress that is appropriate for you and your circumstances, that enhances your work and fits with a sensible work–life balance.

Ultimately it is all about balance and checking that the stress or pressure is neither too great nor continues for too long, and that it is within your control to a great extent. The level of pressure that people can tolerate at work varies greatly between individuals, and also within the same individual when they have other types of stress occurring in their lives, such as divorce or moving house.

Managing pressure at work as an individual is not primarily about 'stress management', although it includes ways of dealing with stress. It is fundamentally about recognising the importance of self-management, which includes the following:

- being clear about your vision, role and purpose
- having an 'uncluttered' mind
- monitoring your quality of life from your personal perspective
- actively engaging in lifelong learning
- putting self-development into practice
- developing a closer 'fit' between your purpose at work and the organisation in which you are working
- good interpersonal skills – relating to your colleagues, patients, managers and others at work, and your partner and family at home.

Increasing patient demand has caused greater stress and time pressures for doctors, nurses and other clinicians and managers. Patients and the public have raised expectations, there is more monitoring and oversight of professionals' work, and there has been some loss of clinical autonomy as a result of Government directives and their execution by managers acting on the Government's behalf. Health professionals try to meet the goals that are shelled down upon them – to provide continuity of patient care, to be more proactive in health promotion, to collaborate more with members of their own team and other agencies, and to take a greater part in health planning and commissioning of care and services for their community. They are becoming increasingly dissatisfied with the lack of time that they have for direct patient care.[12]

Box 1.5: Factors associated with stress at work

Management and culture
- Unclear vision, goals and objectives
- Deficient two-way communication
- Poorly trained managers
- Inadequate training and development of staff
- Lack of humanistic values
- Closed and dishonest culture

Relationships at work
- Unfair and inconsistently implemented personnel and management policies
- Unfair systems for dealing with interpersonal conflict and grievance

Job design
- Inferior training and resources
- Poorly defined role and responsibilities
- Mismatch between workload and individuals' skills, knowledge and ability
- Poor job design

Employee contributions
- Lack of involvement in the change process
- Poor consultation

Physical factors
- Inappropriate environment, with excessive levels of noise, heat or cold

Adapted from Howe[13]

It is important to understand work-related stress and ill health in relation to the whole healthcare organisation. Interventions to manage pressure should be put in place throughout an organisation (e.g. the practice, primary care organisation or trust). Until recently, most interventions tended to focus on stress (the signs, symptoms and effects in individuals), as well as on strategies to use in order to manage stress. This narrow approach ignored the performance implications and the usefulness of positive pressure for achievement.

Box 1.6: A study of stress levels in hospital-based staff[14]

A study of stress in employees in NHS hospital trusts surveyed staff in the mid- and late-1990s using the General Health Questionnaire-12 (GHQ-12) scale to measure their levels of stress. Just over a quarter of employees were found to be suffering from significant levels of stress. Managers were more likely to have higher stress levels than ancillary workers. The rate of psychiatric distress among NHS staff was substantially higher than that recorded among UK

continued overleaf

employees in general. Larger hospital trusts tended to experience higher levels
of stress. The work characteristics which seemed to account for the differences
in stress levels between employees were high work demands, low level of influence over decisions, poor feedback on performance, and conflict between an
employee's various roles.

Not all pressure is productive, and therefore we need to use preventative and
restorative strategies to deal with stress. You can adopt intervention programmes at different levels – at the level of the individual, at the organisational
level, or at the interface between the individual and the organisation (practice,
directorate or trust). These interventions can be classified according to the target
of the intervention, which may be aimed at the individual, the individual–
organisational interface or the organisation.[15] The commonest form of intervention is probably that of stress-reduction activities for individual members
of staff (e.g. stress management training), which are perceived by employers
to be less organisationally disruptive than alternative approaches. However,
successful programmes for managing stress in an organisation will involve
targeting all three dimensions.

Box 1.7

A recent guidance booklet from the Health and Safety Executive concludes that
ill health is a constant concern that requires the expense and inconvenience of
short- or long-term measures for temporary cover. The guidance advises the
NHS to ensure that further illness is not generated in the workplace as a result
of stress. 'A burnt-out workforce is an unproductive workforce ... it is in no one's
interest to find themselves in ... the situation of being unable to cope with the
strains placed upon them.'[16]

Establishing a positive corporate culture is also important in the NHS, where
employers and managers are responsible for the welfare and well-being of
the workforce. Practices or directorates, trusts or other primary care organisations should look to establishing management standards for communicating
with staff, introducing proactive measures to reduce stress-provoking factors within the organisation, acting to boost staff morale, and maintaining
rehabilitation programmes for those in whom they have failed to prevent
stress. The culture of the NHS as an organisation should enable employees
to feel that they can report feeling stressed or suffering from stress-related
illnesses.

In England, Standard 1 of the Mental Health National Service Framework requires that 'health and social services promote mental health for all' and that 'action is taken to address the discrimination and exclusion experienced by people with mental health problems'.[17] Local-health promoting units remind employers that people who are satisfied with their jobs are more productive, and therefore their organisation will be more effective.[18] Mental health policies in workplaces should aim to:

- promote the well-being of staff
- support staff who are returning to work after experiencing a mental health problem
- adopt a positive approach to employing staff who are either experiencing or have experienced mental distress.

2

Beating stress: understanding why, what and how stress occurs

What is stress?

Stress is difficult to define, as it is such a vague word and everyone interprets it differently. Stress is equivalent to a person's perception of the pressure upon them, or the 'three-way relationship between demands on a person, that person's feelings about those demands and their ability to cope with those demands'.[19] Stress reflects the lack of fit between the person and his or her environment, and is an intervening variable between a stimulus (factors provoking stress for a person) and the response (the effects of stress on that person).[5]

Stress may result either from stressful events themselves or from your perception of them. A particular event or task may be very stressful for you on one day but not on another – it all depends on how you are feeling and what other pressures are being exerted on you.

In general, stress occurs in situations where the demands on you are high, your control over those demands is limited, and you have inadequate support or help.

Different occupations have their own particular stresses that are intrinsic to the nature of the job (e.g. the pressure to sell and remain financially solvent in business, or the stress of caring for ill people with limited resources in the health professions). Job insecurity is a potent source of stress. A person's role in their employing organisation may be stressful, too (e.g. taking responsibility for employing or managing other people, uncertainty about what is required, or being under-skilled for the responsibilities of your post).

Extent of stress felt by managers and health professionals

In a recent survey, 20% of general practitioners in the UK reported that their work-related stress was 'both excessive and unmanageable', and a further

60% described their work-related stress as 'excessive but manageable'.[20] More than a quarter of those responding were considering a career change outside general practice 'very' or 'fairly' seriously, and nearly half would not recommend general practice to a medical student or junior doctor.

One study of NHS staff compared their responses to the General Health Questionnaire-12 (GHQ-12) with those of workers from other organisations.[21] The percentages of those scoring as *stressed* were as follows:

- manufacturing managers   23%
- administrative staff   24%
- doctors employed by hospital trusts   25%
- professions allied to medicine   27%
- nurses   28%
- GPs   30–48%
                                                      (varies between studies)[22]
- NHS managers   33%.

In another study that looked at the prevalence of job strain among doctors and staff working in primary care,[14] the percentages of the various types of staff scoring as *stressed* according to the GHQ-12 scale were as follows:

- doctors   30%
- managers   30%
- district nurses   27%
- health visitors   24%
- practice nurses   22%
- clerical staff   18%
- receptionists   17%.

Causes of stress

Stress emanates from the following:

- internal sources – arising from within the individual
- external sources – arising from the environment
- a mixture of internal and external causes.

Table 2.1 lists the psychosocial and organisational hazards to which employees may be exposed at work. These hazards are derived from the content and context of their work. The ten broad categories apply just as much to conditions in the NHS as to those in any other type of workplace.

Change and turmoil.

Table 2.1: Summary of psychosocial and organisational hazards[23]

Category	Hazardous conditions
Content of work	
Job content	Lack of variety or short work cycles, fragmented or meaningless work, under-use of skills, high levels of uncertainty, continuous exposure to people at work
Workload/work pace	Work overload or underload, high degree of time pressure, continually subject to deadlines
Work schedule	Shift working, inflexible work schedules, unpredictable hours, long or unsociable hours
Control	Little participation in decision making, lack of control over workload or pace or shift working, etc.
Environment and equipment	Inadequate, unsuitable or poorly maintained equipment, poor environmental conditions (e.g. lack of space, poor lighting, excessive noise)
Social and organisational context of work	
Organisational culture and function	Poor communication, low levels of support for problem solving and personal development, lack of definition of (or agreement on) organisational objectives
Interpersonal relationships at work	Social or physical isolation, poor relationships with superiors, interpersonal conflict, lack of social support
Role in organisation	Role ambiguity, role conflict, responsibility for people
Career development	Career stagnation and uncertainty, under-promotion or over-promotion, poor pay, job insecurity, low social value to work
Home–work interface	Conflicting demands of work and home, lack of support at home, dual career problems

The major sources of stress for general practitioners appear to include the following:[9,24]

• excessive working hours
• administration
• Government-inspired changes
• the emotional burden of patient care
• worry about complaints
• conflicts between career and personal life.

Disturbing life events

Significant changes in your life or lifestyle can create additional stress. These may concern disruption of your relationships (e.g. through marriage, divorce, bereavement, births, etc.) or changes in your circumstances (e.g. moving house, changing job, retirement). The level of stress that is incurred by a particular event depends on how you view that event and how well you are able to absorb or manage stress. If you experience more than one such event at the same time, the amount of stress resulting from each of them quickly adds up to serious levels that may take some coping with and that will affect you considerably.

What health professionals and managers find stressful

The causes and sources of stress vary between different individuals and different organisations. The types of factors that people working in the health service describe most commonly as causing them to feel work-related stress[25–27] include the following:

- patients' inappropriate expectations of what care and services can be provided and when
- interruptions when they are trying to get work done
- paperwork and administration
- conflict between the demands of a career and family life
- interference with their social life
- the emotional toll of dealing with death and dying
- making mistakes in patient care or work in general, or fearing that they might make mistakes
- fear of litigation
- work/demand overload.

Box 2.1: The emotional demands of dealing with severe illness or social problems

You need to develop the right balance between empathy and professional detachment, to call upon colleagues' support and develop sufficient emotional resilience yourself (*see* page 35).

Doctors, nurses and therapists often mentioned the emotional toll taken by caring for patients with severe or terminal illnesses or severe social problems, in one study of stress and strain issues in general practice.[13] Some recognised that they needed to strike a balance between empathy and detachment in order to cope with the emotional demands. Others commented that becoming emotionally detached can be stressful in itself if it leads you to think that you are not doing enough for patients. Formal and informal support from colleagues, family and friends helped many of the respondents to cope with their distress caused by these types of cases.

continued overleaf

> Those who appeared to cope best with the emotional demands were those who were able to compartmentalise their feelings and adopt a sympathetic and warm approach to the patient as appropriate, while maintaining sufficient professional detachment to avoid the consequences of over-involvement.

Work-related violence is a particular cause of stress that is too frequent within the NHS. There are around 65 000 recorded violent incidents experienced by health service staff each year. Successive British Crime Surveys show that the number of violent incidents at work is increasing across society as a whole. The NHS has a 'zero tolerance campaign' to reduce the numbers of incidents of violence against NHS staff by one-third. This involves working closely with the police to formulate and implement local crime and disorder strategies.

Box 2.2:   Dealing with difficult patients

Dealing with difficult patients has been identified as a cause of stress for NHS staff in one study.[9] Difficulties tend to be divided into rudeness or abuse and sometimes physical assault on the one hand, and inappropriate demands for care on the other. The stress of dealing with difficult patients was reported to originate from the additional workload and the emotional strain on staff.

Many of those interviewed had developed personal and team strategies to reduce the risks of abuse and assault and to minimise the effects of stress on their self-esteem.

Effects of stress on a person

Stress at work does not happen in a 'vacuum'. It is multifactorial – pressures and problems at home often overflow into how someone feels and performs at work, and the effects of stress at work are often taken home and unfairly dumped there.

Stress can affect anyone. It often goes undetected or unacknowledged by the sufferer him- or herself. They may have been warned by others to 'slow down', but delighted in ignoring such advice and pushing themselves on regardless.

Stress is a very real problem that leads not only to a range of psychological consequences, such as anxiety and depression, but also to a range of physiological consequences, such as hypertension and an increased risk of cancer and coronary heart disease.

Signs and symptoms of stress

Physical signs and symptoms include the following:

- feeling tired most of the time
- sleeping difficulties (too little, too much, or poor quality)
- constipation and diarrhoea
- headaches and other aches and pains
- nausea or 'feeling sick'
- high blood pressure
- skin disorders
- heart racing, night-time sweating
- poor appearance (hygiene, clothing, grooming).

DISTRESS   FUNCTIONING

Responses to stress.

Behavioural signs and symptoms include the following:

- inability to sit still
- frequent crying
- doing more work – there is never enough time
- being constantly 'on the go'
- avoidance behaviour (e.g. shunting work away)
- increased consumption of alcohol
- using drugs for relief
- having minor accidents
- altered eating patterns (too much, too little, poor nutrition)
- biting fingernails
- loss of confidence
- putting things off, indecisiveness
- under-performing
- being late for work
- spending longer working but getting less done
- being argumentative, irritable
- being accident prone
- overeating
- demonstrating poor judgement
- losing interest in relationships, sexuality, work.

Emotional signs and symptoms include the following:

- frustration
- anxiety
- restlessness
- despair
- irritability
- dread of the future
- feeling angry, hurt, worried or unhappy.

Mental/cognitive signs and symptoms include the following:

- difficulty in making decisions
- difficulty in concentrating
- negative thoughts such as 'I can't win', 'This is awful' or 'I can't cope'
- forgetting things
- reduction in problem solving
- ruminating.

Different people show various proportions and mixes of physical, mental, emotional and behavioural types of symptoms. The more frequently you observe these signs in yourself, and the greater the intensity of the symptoms that you notice, the more important it is to reflect on how you are managing the pressures in your life.

The effects of stress on an individual can be physical (e.g. resulting in heart disease, lowered immunity or cancer), psychological (e.g. resulting in anxiety and depression) or behavioural (e.g. resulting in an unhealthy lifestyle, absenteeism, early retirement or low productivity).

Box 2.3:   General practitioner morale is at an all-time low[28]

A recent survey of 3700 GPs in Scotland found that more than half of them were suffering from low or extremely low morale. Only 11% of respondents rated their morale as high.

Three-quarters of GP respondents thought that their morale had declined over the preceding five years.

Just under half reported that their levels of stress at work had increased in the last five years, and a further third stated that their stress levels had increased significantly.

The GP respondents believed that more funding for support staff, more time with patients, less bureaucracy and less interference from the wider NHS would lead to a better quality of service.

Effects of stress in the workplace

There are profound effects on an organisation where many members of the workforce are suffering from stress. The resulting physical and mental symptoms spill over to affect all aspects of performance at work. Detrimental effects on relationships with others at work can result in the following:

* poor team spirit/teamwork
* breakdown in communication
* too little time for each other, so no deep bonds of friendship or regard are formed
* too little support for each other
* others feeling stressed when in the company of the stressed person.

The outcomes of such stress on the working of an organisation may make it inefficient, and include (to a greater or lesser extent) many or all of the following:

* organisational problems – poor productivity, disrupted procedures, increased errors, slack timekeeping, accidents, thefts
* poor management – resistance to change, poor decision making, lack of creativity, less opportunities for job fulfilment for staff

- low morale – high levels of job dissatisfaction, disloyalty
- manpower problems – increased sick leave, premature retirement, absenteeism, low levels of effort
- poor relationships – animosity, distrust, disrespect, dissatisfied clients
- increased complaints
- poor communication.

When staff leave, they take years of experience with them and they may be expensive to cover temporarily. It will take time and effort to recruit their replacements, who may need time to be inducted into the job as well as further training.

Effects of stress on your home life

The effects of stress damage your relationships with family and friends just as stress at work can adversely affect your relationships with work colleagues. The types of effects that might result from stress in life outside work include the following:

1 deterioration of family and partner bonds if the stressed person is preoccupied with his or her own feelings and appears disinterested in others
2 lack of support and cohesion for the stressed person
3 children/partner feel that they are unimportant compared with the stressed person's work
4 breakdown of family unit
5 adverse effects of behavioural symptoms that make the individual's situation worse and put further strain on personal relationships.

Effects of stress on patient care and the NHS

About twice as many health service staff suffer from stress as do UK employees in general. NHS managers are twice as likely to have psychological symptoms as other UK managers.

Stress can adversely affect the quality of care. Some typical examples might include the following:

- mistakes (e.g. in prescribing, booking appointments, taking messages)
- increased patient complaints
- increased rates of referrals and investigations, if practitioners are less prepared to tolerate uncertainty

- patients' symptoms taken at face value, if practitioners are less searching in their enquiries
- medical notes misfiled or lost, if practice systems are chaotic
- staff less inclined to listen or empathise
- high levels of staff burnout, adversely affecting relationships, effort at work, and depth of commitment to work.

Effects of stress and burnout on performance

People who are under constant pressure who have symptoms of stress and feel overwhelmed cannot give of their best. Stress can get in the way of performance, although a certain level of stress is necessary in order to perform well.

A common misconception is that there is a linear relationship between the extent of demands applied to individuals and their performance at work. Instead, there is an optimum level of demand where the individual is decisive and creative, working efficiently and effectively. After this point performance tails off once a sensible level of demand is exceeded, and the individual then becomes less effective, less decisive, etc., and eventually becomes exhausted and burnt out. Figure 2.1 illustrates this sequence of events and the 'fantasy line' representing perceived performance.[5]

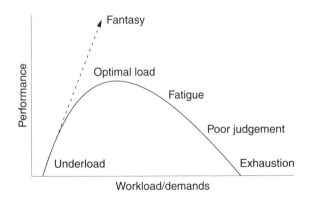

Figure 2.1: Stress performance curve.

Burnout is an intense form of stress that is commonly found among health professionals and those in other caring occupations. It has three independent components, namely emotional exhaustion, low productivity and depersonalisation. It develops when sufferers work too hard for too long under too much pressure (*see* Box 2.4). The types of people who are most vulnerable to burnout are those who are very productive, have high expectations of themselves and set unrealistic targets, while at the same time being reluctant to delegate.

Box 2.4:   Burnout is related to overload from work and inadequacy of resources

One study of burnout and psychiatric disorders in cancer clinicians found that just over a quarter of them scored as *stressed* on the General Health Questionnaire-12 (GHQ-12) questionnaire. Burnout was related to the stress of feeling overloaded, dealing with treatment toxicity or errors and deriving little satisfaction from one's professional status or esteem. Those who were classified as 'burnt out' were more likely to report high levels of stress and low levels of satisfaction from dealing with patients and inadequate resources.[29]

If you ignore the warning signs of burnout and carry on working too hard, you will become increasingly exhausted. Physical symptoms are usually the first stage of burnout, and include fatigue, sleep disturbance, muscular aches and pains, and headaches. This stage is followed by emotional symptoms, such as being noticeably irritable, bored and craving variety, increasingly depressed, and avoiding work. Then 'spiritual' fatigue sets in, where the sufferer loses interest in work, withdraws from other people, ruminates on escape routes from their present life, and feels threatened by demands from work and other people. Their life loses the excitement it once had and becomes a tedious chore.

Exercise 2.1:   Identify your work-based sources of stress

Think of stressful situations that you deal with on a day-to-day basis. What do you consider are the most potent causes of work-related stress for you?

List your top five stressors according to their degree of severity.

1	
2	
3	
4	
5	

Exercise 2.2: Keep a log of the sources of your stress for a week

This is a more detailed version of Exercise 2.1. Instead of just guessing which sources of stress are more frequent or more severe, keep a record of them for several consecutive days – a week if you can manage it – including days when you are at work and off work.

Make several photocopies of the record form on page 28. Fill one in each day for a typical week, recording any significant sources of stress and your usual responses (either good or bad). For example, a 'bad' response or behaviour might be that you drove your car too fast after a row with a member of the practice team, or you lost your temper inappropriately after a succession of interruptions to your work. A 'good' response or behaviour might be that you reorganised a system so that it was more efficient, or you discussed your concerns with others.

Recording seven days' worth should ensure that you get a spread of busy and less pressured days. At the end of the week, review your recordings for all work days and write down your most common stressors at work and your usual responses as a summary. In the same way, summarise the sources of stress from outside work and your usual responses.

Keep at it! If you want a break, leave off doing the log for a day or two and start again later in the week, rather than stopping altogether.

Conclusion
How do you deal with pressure? Start off by considering a few questions.

- Do you feel that you can cope comfortably with all of the demands that are placed on you?
- Are you clear about your responsibilities and boundaries?
- Can you influence the way in which things are done?
- Do you have adequate support?
- Do you feel good about what you do?

The answers to these questions are often interesting and revealing – there may be signs of stress or symptoms of 'burnout' in the responses. You may add further questions.

- Do you have the sense of being continually tired?
- Are you feeling increasingly cynical about work?
- Do you have periods when you lack confidence in carrying out your work?

Notice the ways in which you focus on your behaviours. Do you keep thinking about the 'downside' when you did not do as well as you would have liked? Or do you dwell on your positive progress and reinforce your achievements?

DAILY STRESS LOG AT WORK   Day and date: ....

Source of stress at work: My response:

....

....

....

....

....

....

....

....

....

....

....

....

Comments:

....

....

My overall stress level for today was:

0 1 2 3 4 5 6 7 8 9 10 (circle your reply)

Summary:

3

Beating stress: how to do it as an individual

This chapter examines the issues of pressure that affect us all. We prompt you to consider how you respond to situations, and what you can do for yourself, rather than remaining where you are. In a working and personal environment that is constantly changing, how do you manage to remain clear about who you are and where you are going? How do you use existing self-management skills and competencies and develop others?

Willingness to adapt and change in response to altering circumstances is a vital and unique human quality. By implementing a variety of strategies and techniques, you are enabled to meet challenges, and to be clear and consistent about your own requirements and the boundaries beyond which it is risky to proceed.

How you deal with pressure is a mixture of personal responses, personality and the organisational structures that are in place for managing workplace pressure and stress. Solutions that work well for one person or organisation will not necessarily work as well, or at all, for another.

Box 3.1: What junior doctors want for their work[30]

- *Pay*: sufficient pay to reflect actual working hours, commitment, integrity, lack of job security, and need for improvement in morale.
- *Job security*: a system for redressing the imbalance between the numbers of doctors in training for a specialty and the number of available consultant posts in that specialty.
- *Career progression*: a system for ensuring that there is no financial disadvantage to moving up the junior doctor scale of seniority.
- *Working hours*: rapid implementation of a maximum number of working hours per week that a junior doctor might be expected to work safely.
- *Working environment*: congenial.
- *Family-friendly policies*: including available crèche and nursery facilities.
- *Health and safety*: improved living and working conditions on the hospital site.

Recognising the effects of stress and pressure upon you

The questions posed at the start of the conclusion to Exercise 2.2 are not ones to which demotivated and disempowered people answer 'yes'. Those most affected by stress and burnout features are those whose work involves numerous contacts with people, particularly clients, customers, patients or students.

You should acknowledge the many causes of stress, so that you can then consider what to do to alleviate them. Preventing things getting too bad is the best form of treatment – the earlier the better.

Areas for improvement and planning to prevent stress need to be both internally focused on the individual and also externally focused on your work life, personal life and home life.

Recognising signs of stress and pressure in other people

You might notice changes in a person's personality at work, a marked alteration in their mood or appearance, or a change in their attitude at work. Some of these signs are obvious to all, while others will be hidden. The first step involves taking an opportunity to 'stand back' in order to notice them, once you have become aware of signs of pressure and stress. You will then be in a better position to make decisions about what to do ... and then to do it!

Management and treatment of stress and pressure

Although 'stress' is a subjective experience, you should be aware of the signs and symptoms of stress in order to be able to manage it better. There are three levels of intervention:

1   at primary level – policy level to reduce stressors (e.g. family-friendly work practices)
2   at secondary level – prevention by extending the resources of employees (e.g. self-management and stress awareness training)
3   at tertiary level – treatment focused, for those who have stress-related problems (e.g. counselling, employee assistance programmes).

Interventions to help a person to manage stress more effectively can be undertaken at the individual level, the organisational level, or at both individual and organisational levels.

In general, stress management should include the following three approaches.

*   *Thinking*: more positively; putting things into perspective and thinking longer term rather than short term; being more flexible; finding ways to control your thinking style (see the suggestions later in this chapter).
*   *Behaviour*: talking about your worries to those at work who are responsible for the stress or in a position to alleviate it; seeking support from friends and family; being proactive about controlling stress-provoking factors at work; being assertive; managing your time efficiently.
*   *Health*: achieving a better work–life balance; finding methods of relaxation that work for you; following a healthy lifestyle (eating healthy foods, taking regular exercise, not smoking, limiting alcohol intake).

The evidence for applying interventions to manage stress and pressure

Much research has been conducted on the treatment and management of stress in healthcare professionals[5,25,31] using a variety of physiological, psychological and pharmacological interventions. However, unlike interventions for depression or anxiety, which have a plethora of reliable evidence to support them, a comprehensive search of the literature[32] revealed only one systematic review[33] and one meta-analysis of the treatment of stress.[34]

Although the methodological limitations of much of the underlying research mean that there is little reliable evidence for the effectiveness of these approaches,[35] this does not necessarily imply that stress interventions do not work, but simply that the research to support them is not currently available. As more research is undertaken, evidence may be forthcoming for more of the interventions included in this book.

Despite the lack of concrete research evidence, it is important that stress is managed effectively, and in the following sections we shall outline the current evidence for a range of approaches to stress reduction. We are not advocating any of the interventions that follow – for you as a health professional, manager or member of the support staff in the NHS. We simply present the evidence that does exist, giving you as much information as there is available to make an informed choice about what you might try, in conjunction with your medical adviser.

Psychological treatment of stress

Stress often arises when an individual perceives that their ability does not match the perceived demand.[19] The crucial factor is not their *actual* ability to meet that demand, but their *perceived* ability, and for this reason a range of psychological and behavioural strategies have been used to treat stress.

Autogenic training

This involves a system of very specific autosuggestive formulas that are repeated in a specific pattern, and formulised resolutions that are repeated up to 30 times. Developed by Schultz in 1932, autogenic training draws heavily on hypnosis and yoga. Almost anyone can learn autogenic training by reading a self-help book, and the technique can be mastered in only a few weeks. The evidence for the efficacy of autogenic training is very limited, and one systematic review of eight controlled trials of autogenic training as a means of reducing stress and anxiety reached no firm conclusion about its effectiveness, due to the methodological flaws in the trials.[33]

Stress inoculation training (SIT)[36,37]

This is an individually tailored form of cognitive behavioural therapy that aims to help people to cope with stressful events, and to use existing coping strategies to 'inoculate' clients against ongoing stressors. Clients are informed about the impact and nature of stress and how they may inadvertently exacerbate their levels of stress. They are encouraged to:

- view stressors as problems to be solved
- identify those aspects of their situation that are potentially changeable and those that are not
- break down stressors into specific short-term, intermediate and long-term coping goals.

Stress inoculation training has been shown to be effective in reducing performance anxiety and state anxiety, and in enhancing performance under stress.[34] It has also been used successfully to treat post-traumatic stress disorder.[38]

Cognitive behaviour therapy (CBT)

This focuses on modifying cognitive defences, cognitive reappraisal and developing adaptive behavioural responses. Although a number of research studies have evaluated CBT as a means of stress management, the methodological flaws in these studies, such as the lack of an appropriate control group, mean that there is little reliable evidence to support the effectiveness of CBT.[38]

Exercise

This counteracts the effects of stress mediated through physiological responses by reducing physical complications (e.g. hypertension or coronary heart disease).[27] Active behavioural strategies such as exercise have been found to reduce catecholamine levels in stressed individuals, and they appeal to people under stress as a means of 'releasing tension'. However, there is currently no reliable research evidence in the form of systematic reviews, for the effectiveness of exercise in the treatment of stress.

Stress management training (SMT)

This has been used to treat workplace stress, and is usually offered to groups of staff rather than to individuals. Such training usually includes an educational component, with training in relaxation, goal setting and evaluation and practical skills, such as time management. Participants are encouraged to develop coping behaviours that include changing their environment as well as themselves.[5,25,31] However, there is no standard SMT programme manual, and as each programme is unique, it is impossible to replicate this method in evaluative studies, to generalise to other groups and to assess which are the key components of SMT programmes.

There are no systematic reviews of SMT and so there is little evidence for the effectiveness of these programmes. However, despite the methodological flaws, evaluations of SMT programmes have shown apparent improvements in self-reported psychological and stress-related symptoms, although these are generally short-lived.[31,35]

Mindfulness-based stress reduction (MBSR)

This is a clinical programme which aims to provide systematic training in 'mindfulness meditation' as a self-regulatory approach to stress reduction and management. Despite a growing interest in mindfulness over the past two decades, and claims for its efficacy,[39] there has been little good-quality research. Indeed, there is only one comprehensive review of mindfulness,[40] and this concludes that although the method may hold some promise, the available evidence 'does not support a strong endorsement of this approach at present. However, serious investigation is warranted and strongly recommended.'

Drug treatment of stress

Most cases of stress are self-limiting and will respond adequately to adaptation, problem solving or changing the environment. However, drug treatment may be necessary in cases of severe stress, or where drug and alcohol abuse are complicating factors. A good guiding principle is to treat stress according to the predominant symptoms and suggested regimens are summarised in Table 3.1.[38] Do not be tempted to self-medicate, but see your GP to discuss whether possible treatments are warranted.

Table 3.1:   Pharmacological treatment of stress (Wilkinson *et al.*[38])

Symptoms	Medication	Regimen
Acute stress reaction or adjustment disorder (marked agitation)	Lorazepam*	1 mg orally as required up to 4 mg maximum
	Diazepam*	2–5 mg orally as required, up to 15 mg daily for 1 or 2 days only
Depression with anxiety	Serotonin-specific re-uptake inhibitor (SSRI)	As for *British National Formulary* recommendations; review monthly
Insomnia	Zolpidem**	5–10 mg orally at night
	Zopiclone**	3.75–7.5 mg orally at night

* *Warning*: high potential for dependence.
**Warning*: modest potential for dependence.

Although medication may be useful for the short-term treatment of stress, the adverse effects of many of these drugs, combined with the fact that drugs only treat the symptoms and not the cause of the problem, mean that medication should not be viewed as a long-term cure.

Ideas that you can use to reduce or manage stress and pressure

The word 'management' is often used to describe the external management of something – of a medical condition, professional activities or organisational initiatives (e.g. change management). The following section highlights ideas for individual and personal development in the workplace in the context of 'self-management'. The focus is on ways in which you can use your inner resources. You should aim to find ways to rekindle the purpose you set out with when you were in training, and to examine how you can remain grounded and achieve your capacities.

There are a number of cognitive strategies which you can use to enhance your mental well-being and to manage pressure, people and performance more effectively. As with other self-management approaches, these are simply part of a repertoire of available techniques to be used as and when required, and they need practice and internalisation in order to be most effective.

Your activity map

You are in an *activity trap* if you feel the need to fill your life with constant activities. We crave time for ourselves – but if we get it, we go off out of the door, shopping, walking up a mountain, calling up a friend, cooking, and so on. It has been suggested that modern man is anxiety ridden because the mind is no longer occupied with thoughts of survival (e.g. being eaten, attacked or plundered) and so it seeks stimulation.[41] Because of our need for stimulation we create false enemies and anxieties for ourselves. This may account for the emphasis on filling our lives with countless activities, which can in turn result in our feeling overburdened.

One of the key results of this *activity trap* is that the mind is only working at one speed – a fast one. *Mindful techniques* such as *visualisation* and *mindfulness training* can help you to focus in on a slower speed, and to access energy, intuition, creativity and feelings. With all of these activities flying around, you must find time to let ideas percolate, and in this way you can evaluate what is happening and define your direction in life more clearly. 'Knowledge makes itself known through sensations, images, feelings and inklings, as well as through clear conscious thought. If we do not give ourselves time, these insights will not occur'.[42]

Another issue in finding your ideal work–life balance involves demands on you and your resources. What can you do about the sense of being overloaded, or being pulled in different directions, or having to phone back everyone who has left messages on your answerphone? You need to have both the confidence to grow and the know-how to deal with these challenges. Think about the following questions.

- What are you doing all the time?
- What are you focusing on?
- Where does your energy go?

Exercise 3.1: Draw your own activity map

Take a sheet of A4 paper and divide it into areas on the page, such as a pie-chart, a puzzle, or even graphs, symbols, circles, squares or other shapes or pictures to represent the things with which you are involved – that take up your time and energy. If this is a weekday map, does it change at the weekend? Use symbols and images rather than writing a lot of words. Produce an *impression* of what you do on the piece of paper, rather than a lengthy list of words and sentences. Add up the time you spend on the various activities, as shown in Figure 3.1 below.

An example may look like this:

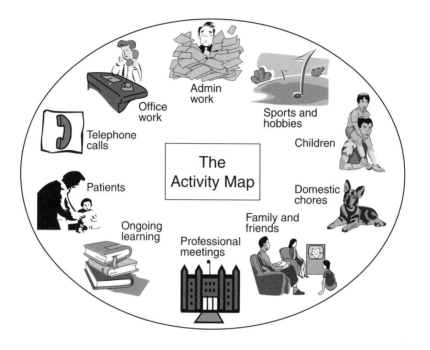

Figure 3.1: Example of an activity map.

continued opposite

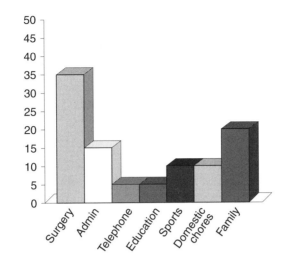

Figure 3.2:   Time distribution of various activities in activity map.

Your activity map is really an activity trap.

Can you see anything that is obviously out of line? Do you have time for yourself? Yes, just you! If you could change anything, what would it be? Are there things which you can swap around, and areas that you can ask other people to help you with (e.g. friends to play sport)? How can you achieve this? Take a differently coloured pen to do this. The more detailed your activity map is, the better you will be able to assess where you are going in your life. Write it down on paper – it's not something that can be made clear in your head.

The vision creates the script

What is the vision you have for yourself or for your profession? You hear a great deal about 'mission statements', and organisations find words to describe the services and values that underpin them. These statements create an impression of what the practice or trust has to offer, to whom and how.

Think back to what your ideals were when you began training and working in the helping professions. What were your hopes and aspirations? What were your dreams? What happened to them? Where are they now? Usually when people consider this challenge, they think not so much in words, but with thoughts, emotions and images. This is the 'vision' that you create for yourself and the world around you.

Establishing 'The Vision'

In May 1961, John F Kennedy, then President of the USA, declared 'We will put a man on the moon before the end of this decade'. This seemed an incredible idea at the time. Only two years earlier a satellite, Sputnik, had been sent into the atmosphere of the earth. Subsequently Juri Gagarin was the first man to enter space. But a man on the moon? Surely not! Nevertheless, this vision motivated and encouraged people from all manner of enterprises to get going. Nuclear scientists and mathematicians, builders and artists, all began to plan and consider how to make this vision a reality. The vision captivated people and was the first step in making it all happen. The people who initiated this work described it as the most enlivening, exciting and stimulating time of their lives. They experienced camaraderie and support and were intensely motivated. Your vision creates your script!

Your vision changes your script

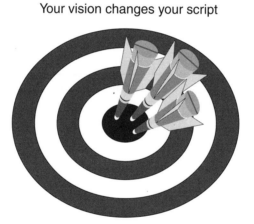

The personal vision forms an anticipatory script
that begins to expand the range of possible actions

Figure 3.3:   The vision creates the script.

Creating the vision: how to do it

You need to be practical and plan carefully in order to translate a vision into something tangible. For example, if you have decided that you want to build a house, you do not go straight out and buy some bricks. You create a vision of the building in your mind, put your vision down on paper, and then plan every detail and measurement. There are choices of a 'ready-made' product or one that you can take a part in creating. Whatever the case, you need to begin at the first stage rather than the last one. How often in your experience do you actually go straight to the building stage and dispense with the planning stage? The result is a project that is abandoned halfway through, or which does not achieve what you had initially hoped for.

If you are constantly in 'crisis' mode, it is difficult to work through the planning stage. You need to find ways of standing back in order to:

- notice
- choose your options
- act.

First, you need to establish the goal or vision in your mind and on paper. Then you will be ready to go and physically create or do it. You may seem to get somewhere faster by skipping the goal setting and planning stages, but without the considered plan it rarely works out effectively. Similarly, you can consider planning in new, creative and highly practical ways at work. Creative planning can be applied to organisational strategies and health at work as well as to managing pressure and reducing stressors.

Developing a vision for yourself at work in the NHS

You might begin by developing a vision of your long-term aims. If your plan is going to inspire you, it must link to some long-term aim which you really want to achieve. You probably have some career goals in mind (e.g. becoming a regional tutor, becoming a lead clinician in a specific field, studying a new skill, taking a lead in staff development, or leading at work in a new way). You probably also have some personal goals (e.g. renovating a derelict cottage, learning a musical instrument, becoming a good skier or tennis player).

Whatever these goals might be, and regardless how long term they are, it is useful to establish a clear framework for their achievement. Your goals may change, but the habit of planning to attain a goal remains an important skill (*see* Chapter 6 for an in-depth approach to long-term planning).

Exercise 3.2: Create your vision for a service

Let yourself imagine what it would be like to be working in an ideal service.

Task 1. What would an ideal service be like for those attending it as a service user? What would they notice? Spend between three and five minutes on this task and write down a brief list of five or so points on what the person using it would notice.

Task 2. What would an ideal service be like for those working in it – as a health professional, a manager or a person in a supportive role? What would they notice? Spend between three and five minutes writing down a brief list of five or so points on what they would notice about this ideal service when working in it.

continued overleaf

When doing both of these tasks, think about the following points.

- What would the atmosphere and response from staff be like (e.g. how would they greet the patients or clients)?
- What would the service, the waiting times and the personal attention be like?
- What would patients notice about the quality and effectiveness of the treatments?
- What about the interrelationships between people?
- What about the space, the seating arrangements, the building, the waiting-room, the clinical rooms, and the other facilities?
- What about the manner in which difficulties would be resolved?
- What about support, career and personal advancement, and training opportunities for those working for that service?

The concept of mental videos

The concept of 'mental videos' concerns the way in which you look at situations and how you think and feel about them. In some ways our mental mechanisms can be compared to scripts, with characters assuming set roles and undertaking particular activities. If you think about the way in which you 'look at' life, you may find that you view the world in many different ways.[43]

If you have a clear vision of what you want and where you are going, you can begin to change the 'internal video'. Changing your mental video means changing your general beliefs about yourself and others, and can lead to altered behaviour and performance. You should challenge the underlying mental videos that affect your behaviour. For example, a behaviour might be 'I rarely put myself forward for promotion'. What might the underlying mental video be? It could be 'I am not really good enough – I am programmed to fail'.

Another good example is to think about how you behave when you become angry and frustrated because you cannot do something on the computer. Your current mental video may be 'I am no good at technical things', but you *can* change the negative way in which you think.

Reframing

Reframing involves taking an event and presenting it in a different way. Instead of viewing something as a 'heart-sink' situation, you can look at it differently.

You can use reframing in an interchange with a time-pressured colleague who is irritated by a request from you for a minor task, saying 'I should have thought that you of all people know about the stress that doing extra paper-work will give me'. Instead of feeling guilty, as your colleague intends, reframe your colleague's frustration as being understandable under the circumstances.

Another example of reframing cropped up at a workshop held at a post-graduate educational venue, well known for its invariably boring lunch menu. When people complained that the centre's only warm meal was baked potatoes, one participant who went there regularly said 'I decided that I would not eat baked potatoes anywhere else but here, so when I see a course advertised, I begin to look forward to eating a baked potato!'.

Exercise 3.3:   How could you reframe the following events for your own circumstances?

- Being criticised directly by a patient or a service user.
- Being told that you are disorganised.
- Feeling that your skills have been devalued.
- Feeling that you have not been as supportive of your colleagues as you might have been.
- Feeling frustrated because you are behind with your work.

(We have not included any answers with regard to the reframing of these statements, as the way in which you reframe them will be individual to you.)

Clarification

This is one of the best strategies that you can use. Seek clarification in every situation – seek and seek again. What about a project or action that you are considering taking on? Clarify the project by converting the concept into a series of clear behaviours. If you decide that you want to study for a new skill, that is still a mental concept. Even if you are committed to this in principle, unless you are aware of the behavioural steps necessary to achieve the concept, it will not happen. First acknowledge what has to be done – you are now at the awakening or awareness stage.

Positive self-talk

You may sometimes find yourself looking at things in a bleak manner, and telling yourself about the negatives and the likely difficulties that you predict will happen if you proceed to do something. Constantly repeating negative views to yourself can lead to further frustration and feeling 'down' about things. Instead, you should adopt positive self-talk, changing from negative to positive words and statements. For instance, instead of saying 'I am worried about something', replace that with 'I am wondering about something'. Instead of saying 'I should', say 'I could'. Seek evidence that refutes your negative thoughts, by looking at times when the negative events did not occur when you were in similar situations.

Table 3.2:   Example of daily record of negative internal thoughts that need turning around

Date	Emotions	Situation	Internal thoughts
	How you feel, how bad it is (0–100, where 0 = least emotion and 100 = most emotion)	What you were doing or thinking about	The habitual thoughts or mental images you have, what your thoughts are, how much you believe each of them (0–100%)
5 May	Tense – 90 Angry – 90 Despair – 75	Dog next door barked for half an hour	I can't stand this. Why can't it shut up? We're saddled with a house that will always be spoiled by that dog barking and we'll never get away from it (80%)
6 May	Panic – 80 Anxiety – 80	Car engine overheating, cold outside and getting dark	I don't know what to do (100%) It's too dangerous to go on, I'll do something to the car (80%) I can't stop here as I'll cause an accident (80%)
10 May	Lonely – 70 Helpless – 60 Unhappy – 90	At work people are grumbling and not trying to make things work	I don't want to be here (100%) I can't leave – I need the money (100%) They don't care, so I have to do everything (90%) I have nothing in common with anyone here (90%)

The notion of self-efficacy

Your effectiveness is linked to the notion that you have of your 'self-efficacy' – that is, whether you believe that you can do something or not. When trying out new things, you need to deal with your 'mental videos' and your general beliefs about what you are doing. Once you have done something, then you can easily do it again, since you have begun to see yourself and your abilities differently.

As your confidence develops, the more you do something, the more you will see your success and the more you will start to alter your beliefs about your own abilities. Then you will do it more frequently and a positive feedback cycle will emerge. When this is reinforced or encouraged through further action, rehearsal and practice, you have started to form a new habit. The factors associated with self-efficacy are highlighted in Figure 3.4.

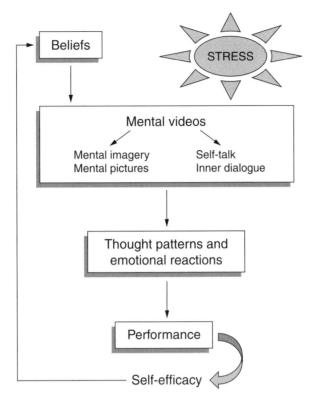

Figure 3.4:   Self-efficacy.

Uncluttering the mind: make time for reflection

The section on the 'activity trap' noted the heightened sense of urgency to 'be busy' all the time. If your mind requires a constant behind-the-scenes 'humming', remember that being still and quiet is often of greater benefit than a flurry of hectic energy.

There are times when you need to sit back, even if only briefly, and gain a different perspective. In the above exercises you learned about some of the cognitive methods of reviewing and reframing. Your mind also needs 'uncluttering' when it is in overdrive. This will result in you:

- having better concentration and focus
- taking time for a 'mental check' and servicing your mind
- clearing the system
- mentally 'de-fragmenting'
- reducing stress.

You might sit quietly and practise some of the other techniques of mindfulness or visualisation described below.

Use the process of self-reflection alongside strategies and tools for personal development in the workplace to consider the following questions.

- Who are you?
- Where have you come from?
- Where are you going?

Mindfulness

Mindfulness is a way of 'being' as well as a technique. It can help ordinary people in stressful everyday situations. It is about being focused in the present moment, rather than being caught up in thoughts or feelings about the past, or in worries or anxieties about the future. Mindfulness is about intentionally paying attention in a particular manner, in a non-judgemental way. There have been programmes using this approach in the USA for the past 15 to 20 years.[39]

The technique of mindfulness distracts your mind from negative or ruminative thoughts. When a person is worrying or looking back, they are 'thinking' about concepts, whereas in mindfulness the person is 'experiencing' the present.

By using mindfulness you register what is happening in this moment, and then you can decide what to do. The frequent practise of mindfulness becomes a general skill or competency. It permits you to evaluate things and then attach priorities to them, rather than rushing to engage in action without purpose. Mindfulness changes your relationship to your thoughts and feelings in general.

Initially, mindfulness originated from work in the area of pain management with patients with intractable pain of long-standing duration. People in chronic pain tended to have a sense of being overwhelmed by the pain, and might wake up in the morning feeling that they had had a bad night. Their internal dialogues would be something like the following: 'This is terrible. I had an awful night, the last days have been bad and I don't know how I will cope with the pain today. I am sure I won't be able to do much and this week will be a write-off.' According to this scenario, the past, the present and the future all gel into one, and the person does not live in the present moment.

Perhaps you too can catch yourself doing something similar – living in the past with a sense of negativity about frustrations or guilt, or alternatively being locked into the past with good experiences and happy memories, without living fully in the present moment. Sometimes you might be looking to the future, hoping for (or fearing) certain outcomes, wondering or worrying – and again failing to make the most of being in the present.

Individuals with chronic severe depression are another group of people who can use mindfulness training to great positive effect. Depressed people often have an over-generalised autobiographical memory. If you ask them to tell you about something that has made them sad, they may reply 'I was awfully sad last year – it was just horrible. It has been such a sad year.' However, other people might respond to that question by saying 'when my pet died' or 'when my partner shouted at me'. Training in mindfulness methods helps chronically depressed people to notice the patterns and cyclical nature of their condition so that they are able to say 'I am still feeling depressed at times, but when I am, I know it will not last for ever'. In learning how to break down their experiences and notice more, they begin to focus on positive aspects of their lives, while living in the present – with both pleasure and difficulty.

Mindfulness is a simple, effective and practical method for restoring balance, becoming more focused and noting things better in order to make more effective decisions. You can do it in a few minutes once you have the skill.

Mindfulness involves the following:

- living in the present moment
- noticing
- awareness
- being grounded
- focused attention
- loving kindness – to yourself (valuing yourself and being non-judgemental).

Exercise 3.4: Try out mindfulness for yourself

- Where would you apply this?
- In what way would it be helpful?
- Who would notice?
- What would people notice about you?

Box 3.2: Being mindful of what makes your job worthwhile

Being mindful of the parts of your job that you enjoy can make up for the every-day aggravations. One doctor recently described 'the times when, however briefly, everything comes together and fits. The unifying diagnosis.... The collateral history from the relative or partner that makes sense of the disparate stories spun by a delirious or demented patient. A brief word of thanks.... The searching look in the eyes of someone hoping for comfort or a cure. The comradeship of colleagues. And last, but far from least, the glorious uncertainty of it all. The knowledge that tomorrow will never be the same as today. That death can be cheated and joy can come as often as despair.'[43]

Visualisation

You know that the mind and the body are linked. When something is worrying you:

- your mouth dries up
- your shoulders and neck feel tense
- you have 'butterflies' in your stomach
- your anxiety makes your heart beat faster.

When walking down the street you may trip up if you realise that people are watching you. Similarly, if you notice yourself being watched, you may find that your body language changes and you become more defensive. What causes these different states to occur? Fundamentally, it is because of the way in which your mind perceives the situation. Two people can see the same event but can be affected quite differently by it.

To counteract negative mental stress, one of the reframing strategies is mental imaging or the running of 'internal videos'.[45] Findings in clinical psychology suggest that positive mental imagery can enhance performance in a wide range of individuals.[44] Mental imagery is one of the most widely researched cognitive techniques used in athletics and sports science,[46] and is slowly working its way into the management literature.[47–49] Visual imagery plays a part in the beliefs and actions concerned with the regulation and interpretation of a person's cognition.[50] People can be enabled to use their imagination both to deal with debilitating past experiences and to work towards positive future occurrences.[51]

Both academic and practical texts have been written about the uses of visualisation and imagery in the fields of medicine,[52–54] personal development and well-being,[55–58] sports science[46] and organisations.[43,49,59,60] Individuals' and organisations' anticipation of events guides their actions. Training packages based on visualisation encourage individuals or organisations to form images or blueprints to guide their action.[61] A person's actions are energised and intensified by their confident expectation of the positive outcomes that they have envisaged.[62,63]

Box 3.3:   Visualisation: the definition

The internal experience of memories, dreams, fantasies and visions. Imagery involves not just visual awareness, but all of the senses.[64]

Associated words: visualise, imagine, fantasise, daydream, pretend.

Consider for a moment a blank videotape. You buy it, record on it, erase it, play it back, forward or re-record on it as often as you like. Your mind has developed in a similar way. When you were born you had a very sensitive blank videotape built into your mind. Images, words and events are recorded on to this tape. You imagine that as you grow older more information is recorded on to this tape. Unlike the videotape, you may forget to erase the previous information. So the videotape in your mind is composed of many layers of words, images, experiences and much more.

When your life's experiences are recorded on to this mind tape, you normally consider that to be fixed, as part of your 'personality'. However, visualisation helps you to challenge the notion that your personality is a set defined structure. Visualisation takes your mind's videotape and allows you to stop the tape, erase some of it, re-record, and so on. People like to feel that what they record on the tape is their decision and not dictated by others. Visualisation allows you to develop a new 'groove' in the brain and to change existing old habits.

Visualisation provides an opportunity to play out a scenario in your mind and cut out part or all of the internal dialogue which is going on. It allows you to relax and to focus, even if only for a few short moments, on a particular situation. Other creative ideas will occur as a result of being there in that moment. These come from that part of your consciousness which is somewhat suppressed by the logical, rational and literal part of your brain. Visualisation will enable you to shut out negative thoughts and feelings and to focus on what you are trying to achieve.

Visualisation allows you to create powerful pathways in your brain and enables you to generate feelings of control, power and success. You can create these feelings in your head. For example, imagine that you are in a boardroom. You can rehearse a speech, you can meet people who support you, or you can include people whom you admire, and you can control access to the room so that you can have anyone you like in there. These feelings will create new pathways in your brain. The more you can do this, the more the ideas about yourself are embedded in your mind. The more that they are embedded, the more you will carry out the behaviour, triggering a positive cycle of feeling, rehearsal and achievement.

Visualisation allows you to do the following.

- It enables you to imagine something new that is important to you, such as a skill or service. Begin with a forward-thinking idea. Put that idea into words and pictures, and then convert the pictures and words into that skill or service. The first stage in creating the life you want is to imagine yourself 5, 10 or 15 years into the future and work backwards. If you want a certain lifestyle in 5 years' time, what do you have to do *now* in order to achieve it? If you wish to go on a different type of holiday, you can use visualisation and imagery to decide, in great detail, on the type of holiday you would like.

- It helps you to sort out your priorities and really connect with what you would like to focus on. Imagine a moment ahead in time – see yourself in 5, 10, or 20 years' time. For example, if you look forward 5 years to a really close relationship with someone, you might realise that to have that wonderful relationship in the future you might have to implement some different behaviours now in order to bring you closer together. Spend more time together to communicate and share your vision. We all have the ability to look forward and to imagine ourselves achieving something like this. Live now, but also create the future you want to see happen. When you have seen what is possible, you can work back to the present and see what you need to change in order to achieve your 1-year vision, 3-month vision, or whatever.

- It allows you to rehearse a situation. Think of any situation in life where you have performed badly or indifferently. What would happen if you had a second chance? For example, what if you had an opportunity to erase the impression in the minds of the interviewers and rerun an interview? You would probably have performed better the second time round. So how much more effective would you be if you had had a chance to rehearse? Then when you encountered the reality, your mind would be predisposed to act automatically. For example, think of an important committee meeting you might have ahead of you. You can rehearse a range of possible scenarios in your mind. Where will you sit if someone else is already sitting at the top of the table? What action will you take if coffee is served while you are making the introductions? Visualisation cannot cover everything that could occur, but by covering as many options as you can think of, you will be relaxed and should be able to cope with any unexpected situation.

- It enables you to enhance a positive belief. If you wish to change a negative belief that you hold, you can test that belief or rate it in a logical way. Look at the different scenarios, and see yourself overcoming your negative belief step by step. Analyse what hard evidence there is to support your negative belief, and try to stick to reality. Change your negative thoughts and behaviours, and take positive action.

- It allows you to achieve a very deep level of relaxation. You can be as creative as you like in achieving relaxation in different parts of your body and using all kinds of strategies to position yourself. Visualisation opens you up to perceiving things differently, almost with 'different parts of your brain', bypassing your normal defences and logical rational thoughts. Images are powerful and can be relaxing. You can achieve this deep relaxation with guided imagery as well as with set imagery (e.g. imagining a pleasant place where you feel contented).

Exercise 3.5:   Try out visualisation for yourself
- Where would you apply this?
- In what way would it be helpful?
- Who would notice?
- What would they notice about you?

Protocol for developing and running a revised 'mental video' through visualisation

The following stages outline the steps you can take to realise the full bene-fits of visualisation. You should spend some time working on each of the various stages. In this way you will become aware of your mind-and-body responses. Focus fully on all of your senses, and link these with your personal vision in the form of your new 'mental video'.

Stage 1: developing a script for the new 'video'

Be aware of all your senses when creating the new script for your 'mental video'. As you develop the new script in the way described previously, the 'video' emerges and becomes more personally relevant. Once the script is clear, it is time to move on to the following stages.

Stage 2: calming breathing

Breathe deeply and take regular deep breaths – this starts the cycle of calming relaxation, which will decrease tension and reduce your levels of physiological arousal. Ultimately this will lead to less generalised tension in your body.

Stage 3: mindfulness

It is time to manage any intrusive thoughts, images and sensations that hamper the calming process. Learn to notice these without becoming influenced by them or caught up by them. Focus on your breathing, take a breath as an anchor point, and disengage from any interference from external or internal sources.

Once this groundwork has been undertaken, it is time to implement the script of the new 'video'.

Stage 4: running the new video

Use a prepared script for the new video that incorporates a scenario relevant to you personally. This might be about establishing a new skill which starts to become 'engrained' in your mind–body system. You will be using imagery-generating areas of your brain and triggering new mental pathways.

Stage 5: embedding the new video

This new script and the process outlined above need to be repeated regularly. By using 'self-talk' and positive affirmation, as well as the sequence of 'trial and success', the new video becomes internalised and embedded. The image of successful achievement affects your thoughts, feelings and performance, and this underpins the positive steps that lead to your new pattern of behaviour.

Support mapping

What are your support structures? Are they within or outside you? Do you have any personal or organisational support, such as mentoring, coaching, peer supervision, support groups, etc.? Do you make enough time for yourself? Are you continually giving to others at work and at home? Does your practice or directorate, trust or primary care organisation fulfil its duty of care as a learning and supportive organisation? Would you notice?

Box 3.4:   Health professionals need adequate practical and emotional support throughout their careers

A study of the impact of job stress and working conditions found that work-related stress triggered the deterioration of junior doctors' mental health throughout their pre-registration year.[65] Their deteriorating mental health was not related to their personality types or whether they had suffered from mental health problems in the past. It was their *perceived* job stressors (e.g. emotional pressure in the job and not being able to meet the demands of patients) that were of more significance than *objective* work stressors (e.g. the number of hours spent working or 'on call' per week). The authors of the study concluded that junior doctors need adequate support and more flexible working arrangements during their early years in hospital, as well as training in coping with occupational stressors.

Developing support structure[66]

Support in managing day-to-day pressures is varied, and is often unique to the individual. Apart from helping to cope with pressure and stress, you can use a variety of support systems to motivate you, to help you to achieve your vision and to inspire you. These resources may be found within yourself (e.g. your mental attitude, positive self-talk, visualising enhanced coping) or elsewhere (e.g. supervision, mentoring, coaching, counselling). How can you go about examining your sources of support?

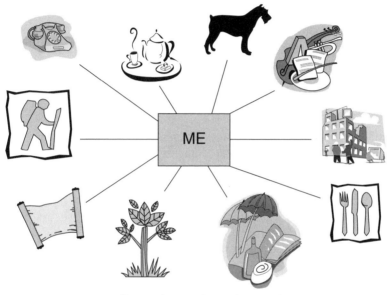

Personal support mapping exercise

Figure 3.5:   Example of personal support map.

Exercise 3.6:   Mapping your support systems

Take an A4 sheet of paper and draw a picture or map of your support systems both at work and at home. In the centre, draw a representation or symbol of yourself. Draw pictures, symbols, diagrams or words around 'you' to represent all of the things and people that support you in learning and being creative at work and at home. These may be the walk to work, books you read, colleagues, meetings, friends, etc. Have you drawn them near to you or far away? Is the link strong and regular or tenuous or distant? Are they supporting you from below like foundations or are they balloons that lift you up? These are simply suggestions – you will find your own way of mapping your support system.

continued overleaf

What impression does your map or picture create? Is this the support that you want? Is it enough? What kind of support is missing? How could you go about obtaining more support? What support is really positive for you (so that you should nurture and maintain it)? What blocks can you actively break down and overcome?

Having examined this map, you may realise things that you would like to change or develop. Using this process, you will be able to refine your awareness of how things are currently and how you might like them to be. As you become more aware, you may consider your choices and actions. You should realise that there are things you can do! From this you can develop specific action plans for how you might improve your support system. The action plan should include *what* you are going to do, *how* you are going to do it, *when* and *where* you are going to do it, and *who* will be involved.

Box 3.5: Support service in community trust promotes general well-being for staff[67]

A well-being project run by one community trust includes confidential counselling as part of its organisational approach. The counselling service is staffed by a dedicated team of people who do not work elsewhere in the trust (thus avoiding conflicts of role), and is based away from other trust services. Other linked initiatives include provision of programmes to teach staff how to cope with or reduce stress by the training and development service, and specific interventions by managers to help staff who are ill. Staff in the trust are encouraged to confront stress-provoking factors in groups and to find ways to improve working conditions. The integrated approach to well-being is executed through the work that the counselling service team does with senior staff from human resources and management to provide a psychological element to their work on strategy and policy development for the trust.

Become more assertive[5]

Being assertive involves expressing your feelings clearly and openly and behaving consistently with those feelings in an honest way. Being assertive is not the same as being aggressive. It is about deciding what you want to do or what you want to happen, judging whether it is reasonable or not, and acting accordingly.

Your natural instinct as a health professional or manager may be to help people. Even those who are hopelessly overworked will often take on extra tasks even though they know it is crazy to do so. Assertiveness in the work context involves your facing up to the fact that everyone has a limit to their time and energy, and politely but firmly refusing to take on extra work if you know that it will cause you to be over-stretched. Refuse to be manipulated by others.

Assertiveness is certainly not about getting what you want all the time, nor is it about being a perfectionist and driving yourself and others into the ground. It is about setting out your own boundaries, and being prepared to stick up for yourself if you think that you are right, while at the same time being willing to reach a compromise with others. You should be able to learn skills to negotiate assertively with everybody – patients, senior and junior colleagues and family members. Assertiveness is about giving and taking in an equitable way.

In order to be successful in being assertive, you need to understand the tricks that others employ in order to get their own way. Some patients can be devious, dropping hints about what they really want but placing the onus on you to decide exactly what it is. This is ridiculous. You have better things to do with your time and energy than play these kinds of games. Faced with this type of patient, state clearly and simply what you think is the best way forward, and refuse to be sidetracked.

If people try to bully you, and persist even after you have told them 'no', don't give in. Giving in just for the sake of some peace and quiet will make things a hundred times worse, and you will feel resentful as well as stressed. Keep saying calmly but firmly 'I don't think you heard me. I'm not prepared to do that.' It is important to resist the temptation to get angry. Disarm the anger of a patient or colleague by acknowledging their feelings and remaining calm, but do not give in.

Passive behaviour in others can be especially difficult to handle, as it is a technique that you may fall for, not wishing to seem to be taking advantage of someone when he or she is down. You are made to feel selfish if you ignore the 'victim's' wishes or hesitant requests. Be careful. You might end up doing what the passive person wants you to do, rather than live with the guilt of pleasing yourself. Respond by stating specifically what you want with a simple explanation. When the next patient needles you by saying 'No one really cares any more about how people feel' or 'I expect it's all my fault', and you feel tempted to reassure them to the contrary, think of the game that they are playing. They are trying to manipulate you. Don't fall for it!

One of the characteristics of a person who is healthily assertive is that they are not afraid to give their opinion. No one should be afraid to express their opinion on a subject they know something about. And not only do you have as much right to be heard as anyone else – you also have the right to change your mind. If you decide that on reflection you do not want to take on a task, do not be afraid to say so.

The potential advantages to you of being assertive are as follows:

* to increase your self-confidence
* to increase control over your emotions

- to establish better relationships with others – people will relate to assertive people more readily than they relate to those who are passive or aggressive
- to increase your self-respect
- to increase others' respect for you
- to achieve satisfactory changes in your work or home situation.

Learn to recognise your non-verbal behaviour patterns from the list in Table 3.3. Think about particular situations at work that you find difficult, and consider whether the body positions that you are adopting are mainly 'passive', 'assertive' or 'aggressive'.

Table 3.3:   Non-verbal behaviour: the body language that gives you away

Passive	Assertive	Aggressive
Covers mouth with hand	Direct eye contact	Gesticulates expansively
Looks down at the floor	Head erect	Clenched/pounding fists
Constant shifting of weight	Descriptive hand gestures	Finger pointing
Fiddles (e.g. with clothing)	Emphasises key words	Hands on hips
Rubs head or parts of body	Steady, firm voice	Rigid posture
Frequent nodding of head	Open movements	Strident voice
Throat clearing	Relaxed	Stares others down

Are you consistent? Do you behave differently at work to how you behave at home or in another setting? Could you change your non-verbal behaviour and the signals which you give out so that you behave more consistently?

What you can do to be more consistently assertive

1 Be treated with respect.
   - Tell others what you want and need, and what you like and don't like; express positives first and negatives second.
   - Take pride in your appearance and believe in yourself.
2 Have and express feelings and opinions.
   - Use the 'broken record' technique, calmly repeating your original statement (at an appropriate time and place).
   - Let others know what you are feeling; your vulnerability and trust in others will encourage them to confide in you, too.
3 Be listened to and taken seriously.
   - Match your body language to your assertive message (i.e. remain calm and serious, avoid frivolous quips and use direct eye contact).
   - Back up your proposals with well thought out reasons for changes.
   - Initiate and get involved in conversations; don't wait for others to approach you first.

4   Set your own reasonable priorities.
    •   Set your own goals; dismantle barriers to achieving your goals.
5   Say 'no' without feeling guilty.
    •   Use simple, direct language.
    •   Deflect other people's attempts to distract you from your purpose;
        acknowledge that you have heard the other person's viewpoint and
        repeat your response.
    •   Distance yourself from problem situations until you get a handle on
        what is going on – and until you can be adequately prepared with a
        considered response.
    •   Do not lose your self-control and become angry or ill-tempered.
6   Choose not to assert yourself.
    •   Try 'active listening' – listen, clarify, summarise and paraphrase a
        speaker's words in order to improve your understanding of their
        meaning and your rapport.
7   View your needs as being as important as those of others.
    •   Learn to recognise the control tactics that others are using, and be
        ready to counter them; interrupt back, use flattery, engage them as
        advisers, and ask for information if you are excluded from a conversation
        by cryptic remarks.

Tips for assertiveness

1   Say '*no*' clearly, and then move away or change the subject. Keep repeat-
    ing '*no*' – do not be diverted.
2   Be honest and direct with everyone.
3   Do not apologise or justify yourself more than is reasonable.
4   Offer a workable compromise and negotiate an agreement that suits you
    and the other party.
5   Pause before answering '*yes*' if you will regret it later. Delay your response
    and give yourself more time to think by asking for more information.
6   Be aware of your body language and keep it as assertive as possible.
    Match your tone to your words (don't smile if you are giving a serious
    message).
7   Use the 'broken record' technique, persistently repeating your message
    in a calm manner to someone who is trying to pressurise you to do
    something you do not want to do. Don't be side-tracked.
8   Show that you are listening to the other person's point of view and
    giving them a fair hearing.
9   Practise expressing your opinion and rights, rather than expecting
    other people to guess what you want.
10 Don't be too hard on yourself if you make a mistake – everyone is human.

11   Be confident enough to change your mind if that is appropriate.
12   It can be assertive to say nothing.

Keep practising assertiveness until it comes naturally. Other people are often unaware of their own behaviour, and your assertive response to an aggressive person may make them realise how they have been behaving. Be aware that if you are angry, it is unlikely that you will manage to be assertive. Challenge people who are sulking, and invite them to tell you whether they have a problem. If they deny that they have a problem, treat them normally and don't mention the matter again.

Exercise 3.7:   Work through the stages of assertiveness

Think of an example of a situation at work that occurred during the last few days in which you behaved passively or aggressively, and now wish that you had been more assertive. Write down your answers below.
    Describe the situation.

*   Who was involved?
*   Where did the incident happen?
*   What triggered the episode?
*   How did you behave? Were you pushy, shy, obnoxious, uncompromising?
*   How did the other person respond?
*   How well did you communicate your feelings?
*   Did you handle any conflict well?
*   What was the outcome of the exchange?
*   What should you have done or said?

Conclude this exercise by listing below the people at work or outside work with whom you intend to be more assertive, and what you expect the outcome(s) to be.

I intend to be more assertive with:	Likely outcome(s):
1	
2	
3	
4	
5	

Career planning[5,68]

The lack of a clear career structure is a well-recognised cause of stress in any workforce – this applies to general practitioners, hospital consultants and primary care nurses as well as to many managers and support workers. Many people working in the NHS find that they reach the top of their specialties within several years of entering practice, and that there is then a flat career structure with no obvious route to promotion. NHS managers may think that they have a career structure, only to find that the NHS reorganises and changes such that there is no obvious career progression and they need to transfer to a different pathway in another setting.

If you are not working in your chosen career specialty, you are less likely to find your job satisfying and more likely to be stressed.

Too much or too little work, over-promotion and under-promotion can all cause stress, so you should seek the right job match for you – both now and in the future, when your requirements change as you mature and progress.

In the past you may have made the most of opportunities as they came along, rather than taking control and finding the best match of career for your own needs and preferences. The Workforce Development Confederations and other professional bodies are starting to take more responsibility for providing careers information and guidance, and you can find out a great deal from the World Wide Web (e.g. www.nhscareers.net).

Career planning is about career growth, and the pathway along which you learn more about yourself, the facts about the options open to you, the implications of the alternative posts in terms of training, career progression, workload, etc., how to gain qualifications or equip yourself educationally for your preferred posts, how to manage the transition period while taking up new posts, and subsequently how to review and develop your career.

It is likely that as you progress through your career you will want to vary your role and responsibilities, take up new interests at work and specialise in one or more defined areas. For example, you might want to alter the proportion of time you spend on teaching and service work. You need to feel supported by the organisation in which you work to be enabled to change over time. Such change will allow you to become re-energised and enjoy your job.

If you wish to switch careers or combine a substantial new post with your current job, you should plan ahead and aim for a gradual transition rather than an impulsive change. Your previous experience should have paved the way for you to have a good understanding of the types of work and ways of working that suit you. The more the different components of your current career overlap and you can transfer your various skills and strengths over to the chosen post, the easier it is to break new ground from your relatively confident position.

Get the right balance in your job.

Think ahead and make positive plans for retirement, well ahead of when you expect to retire, by financial planning and gathering information about opportunities for further career development. People are now thinking of retiring earlier – the happiest people seem to be those who are enjoying the era of life in which they are at present. By the time they are 50 years old, people have more self-knowledge and are more aware of their boundaries, what makes them happy and satisfied, and how they like working, and they can guard against what overloads or upsets them.

Understanding your own career preferences and style

You cannot make a rational career choice without understanding the 'inner you' and what you have to offer. Your career and personality match is very important, as well as your personal preferences for the balance between work and leisure, work and income, degree of responsibility, type of work, and extent of interaction with people.

Eight career anchor categories have been identified by Schein[69] and used to increase people's insights about their strengths and motivation in career development. Consider what is the one feature about you and your job that you would not give up – no matter what. Is it:

- technical or functional competence
- general managerial competence
- autonomy or independence
- security or stability
- entrepreneurial creativity
- service or dedication to a cause
- pure challenge?

People define their self-image in terms of these traits, and you can come to understand more about your talents, motives and values, as well as which of these is so important to you that you would not give up those facets if you were forced to make a choice.

Box 3.6:   Remember your career anchors

Remember what attracted you into your current post. What was your dream when you began your training? Where is that dream now? One GP registrar said of his career choice of general practice 'It gives me flexibility with my working arrangements. I also enjoy being able to follow patients through and untangle whether their problems are physical, psychological or social.'[70]

Careers information, guidance and counselling[68]

To make a rational career choice you need *careers information* that gives you the facts – in other words, the provision of written and/or verbal information about career opportunities, including the number and type of posts available at a particular level and in a particular specialty, and details of the qualifications and training necessary. *Careers guidance* is more personal and directive, and provides advice within the context of the opportunities that are available. It is useful for those who have not made a career decision or who have decided on their career goal but are unaware of the best way of achieving it. *Career counselling* is a more intensive process that requires specialist skills. Ideally, career counselling builds on careers advice or guidance, appraisal and assessment, and pastoral support. It includes the recognition and analysis of a person's strengths and weaknesses with regard to available career options. Career counselling involves a facilitatory approach for students or doctors who are uncertain of their career direction, or who have specific career problems (e.g. those who have a health disability, or whose career is constrained by personal circumstances, or who seem to be unsuited to their current post).

Achieve the work–home balance that suits you

The pressures that arise from conflicts between health professionals' careers and their home and family lives have been highlighted earlier in this book. Whether you experience such conflicts will partly relate to your ability to keep the demands of work under control. One study of hospital consultants subdivided their approach to the interactions between their career and family lives into the following three strategies:[71]

- *career dominant*: where the doctor had a continuous and full-time career with a reduced family life
- *career and family life segregated*: where the doctor had a continuous and full-time career with family roles organised so as to enable the doctor to have more time to devote to his or her career
- *accommodating career*: where the doctor's involvement in work was reduced in some way to allow him or her more time for family roles.

In the study,[71] women consultants reported that the *segregated* strategy was the most successful in terms of both family and career, whereas male consultants found this strategy less satisfying for family life. Unsurprisingly, both male and female consultants classified the career-dominant strategy as being good for their career and bad for family life, and the accommodating career strategy as being good for family life and bad for their career.

So far, women doctors have tended to select a less career-dominated life, as the numbers who opt for less than full-time working demonstrate (*see* Box 3.7).

> **Box 3.7:**   Switch to part-time working among female GPs[72]
>
> There has been a strong trend among women GPs to work less than full-time. In 1991, 79% of women GPs in England worked full-time, whereas by the year 2001, only 57% did so. Similarly, more male GPs are working part-time, with 98% working full-time in 1991 compared with 93% in 2001. The popularity of job sharing has fallen from 6% of female GPs in 1995 to 4% in 2001, presumably as it has become easier to obtain a part-time post.

Seek medical help if and when you are ill

Doctors are reluctant to seek help from other doctors or to take time off work when they are ill. Most doctors are registered with a GP, but their consultation rates are very low compared with the rest of the general population. Self-prescribing is common among general practitioners and hospital-based doctors.

It can be difficult to get access to a GP at times that suit your own working pattern. Many doctors do not feel that they can trust occupational health services for NHS staff to maintain confidentiality about sensitive problems such as work-related stress or substance misuse.

Doctors have a high threshold for taking sick leave. In one study,[73] male and female doctors took one-third to half of the amount of sick leave taken by nursing managers (head nurses and ward sisters), while nursing managers took far less sick leave than nurses. Doctors tend to work through illness even when they feel too unwell to carry out their work to the best of their ability. Sometimes colleagues put pressure on the sick professional to return to work too early.

> **Box 3.8:**   The culture of general practitioners' care of their own health[74]
>
> Doctors are reluctant to seek help in the normal way when they become ill.
>
> Doctors' perceived need to portray an unrealistically healthy image is stressful and a barrier to appropriate self-care.
>
> The working arrangements of general practitioners reinforce a culture in which their own and colleagues' distress is overlooked .... In reality, influences such as a sense of conscience to provide a service for patients, loyalty to partners, difficult relationships within partnerships, precarious sickness insurance arrangements and poor locum availability may contribute to neglect of self and partners.

So it is important to find a general practitioner you trust, resolve to consult him or her whenever it is appropriate, and resist your urge to treat or diagnose yourself for the types of circumstances when you would expect a member of the public to consult their own GP.

If you do have a serious health problem or a minor illness which means that you cannot work effectively, take sick leave – even if this means colleagues will be left to carry your workload. In the long run it is in everybody's best interest!

The cycle of personal change: practice and reinforcement

You need to embed the new techniques that you have read about in this chapter, so that they are 'common practice' for you. As with most things you do, learning takes place most effectively through practice and doing.

In order to run the different, new script, you need to plan carefully. Begin by implementing your 'new script' within specific areas where there is likely to be little resistance (e.g. in relating to a new patient or a distant contact, rather than a close associate, a member of your immediate team or a family member).

For any effective intervention such as a stress reduction programme, there are four major components:

1   information, designed to increase awareness and knowledge
2   development of self-regulatory skills, whereby informed concerns are translated into effective habits
3   opportunities for guided practice in applying the skills that have been taught
4   enlisting and creating social supports.[75]

So reflect on your chosen methods for beating stress in your life and ensure that you have enough information, opportunities to develop and apply skills and support – to really make a difference to how you feel.

4

Beating stress at work in the NHS: what teams can do

A team is more than a group of people working near to each other.[76] A team has a defined organisational function and identity (e.g. to deliver healthcare to a specific population), and shared objectives or goals (e.g. to provide high-quality patient care). The team members must have interdependent roles which they co-ordinate with each other in order to get the work done.

An effective team is more than a team that performs well – it is one that performs well *and* which has team members who are satisfied and not stressed, has low turnover and absence rates, and is viable – that is, the team can continue to work together.[76]

Teamworking can enhance both the job satisfaction of employees and their level of commitment to the organisation. Self-managing teams which have high levels of employee involvement and autonomy are more likely to thrive, and such teams can lead to better performance and productivity. They should have sufficient autonomy to plan and manage all aspects of their work, including setting goals, allocating work among team members, deciding on work methods, obtaining and evaluating measures of work performance, and selecting and training team members.[76]

Box 4.1

The importance of the team's culture in determining whether staff members experience stress from work has been confirmed by one in-depth study of 81 general practices, which showed that 40% of practice staff in 10 practices scored as stressed (according to their responses to the GHQ-12 scale), while at the other end of the continuum, 10 practices had less than 10% of practice staff who scored as stressed.[9]

You may find that a structured review of the way in which you manage patient throughput in your practice or workplace detects many inefficiencies in your systems that are relatively easy to put right. Some involve better time management as individuals and as a team, while others involve more understanding of each others' roles and responsibilities, so that you work together in a more co-ordinated way.

One study[77] found that many stresses are created or perpetuated by practice policies that are within the power of those concerned and their supporting teams to put right. Examples include the following:

- overbooking patients
- starting surgeries late
- accepting commitments too soon after surgeries were due to finish
- making insufficient allowances for the numbers of extra 'emergency' patients
- booking at consultation rates that are too fast
- allowing inappropriate telephone or other interruptions.

Poor teamwork appeared to contribute to increased sickness-related absenteeism in one study of hospital-based doctors, so investing in the development of teams and effective team leaders makes organisational sense.[73]

Encouraging a well-functioning team

With good facilitation, primary care teams can work together to overcome stress through improved teamwork, better communication and mutual support. Being a member of a well-functioning team reduces individuals' stress levels.

The more that someone's job has the following enriching work characteristics, the more likely employees are to be satisfied, motivated and mentally healthy:[76]

- job autonomy/individual's decision-making authority
- limited pacing of jobs undertaken
- skill variety and opportunity to develop new skills
- feedback about performance
- carrying out a whole task and a meaningful job
- reasonable workload levels
- clear goals, and individuals being clear about their own roles
- consistency with regard to what is expected and absence of 'role conflict'
- positive relationships with colleagues.

Most of the characteristics listed above for individuals are dependent on the organisation and enveloping team. If one or more of the factors is not present, then there will be negative effects on individual team members. The value of teamworking is enhanced if team members co-operate and collaborate to achieve the team goals and work in an interdependent way.

Box 4.2: Emotional intelligence

Emotional intelligence has been recognised as a skill that helps people to work together in harmony.

   The concept of emotional intelligence has been much discussed in the USA. It has been described as 'a type of social intelligence that involves the ability to monitor one's own and others' emotions, to discriminate among them, and to use the information to guide one's thinking and actions'.[78,79]

   Emotional intelligence has five domains:

- *self-awareness*: observing yourself and recognising a feeling as it happens
- *managing emotions*: handling feelings so that they are appropriate, realising what is behind a feeling, and finding ways to handle fears, anxieties, anger and sadness
- *motivating oneself*: channelling emotions towards a goal, emotional self-control, delaying gratification and stifling impulses
- *empathy*: being sensitive to others' feelings and concerns, and appreciating others' perspectives and how they feel about things
- *handling relationships*: managing emotions in others, and social skills.

Characteristics of good teamworking

Your team is more likely to function well if it: [80]

- has clear team goals and objectives
- has clear lines of accountability and authority
- has diverse skills and personalities
- has specific individual roles for members
- shares tasks
- has regular communication within the team, both formally and informally
- has full participation by team members
- confronts conflict
- monitors team objectives
- gives feedback to individuals
- gives feedback on team performance
- has external recognition of the team
- has two-way external communication between the team and the outside world
- offers rewards for the team.

A team leader with a democratic style enables a team to function well, and encourages change rather than imposing it.

Box 4.3:   What predicts the effectiveness of primary healthcare teams? [81]

A study of 68 primary healthcare teams in the UK found that team size, tenure and budget-holding status did not predict team effectiveness. The most effective teams had clear objectives, encouraged participation by their members, emphasised quality and supported innovation.

Good communication between GPs and their staff can reduce stress and improve performance. The following are needed:

- regular staff meetings – which managers and staff endeavour to attend
- a failsafe system for passing on important messages
- a way to share news so that everyone is promptly notified of changes
- a culture in which team members can speak openly without fear of being judged or reprimanded
- opportunities for quieter members of the team to contribute
- the giving and receiving of feedback on how your role in the team is working out
- giving others praise for their achievements
- opportunities for team members to point out problems and suggest improvements
- everyone to be part of, and own, the decision making.

Communication is usually poor if a team lacks stability, or if single disciplines work in an isolated way. In one study, some of the senior doctors were the worst offenders with regard to failing to communicate with others in the team. Power and status issues within a team can interfere with good communication.[82]

Innovations are more likely in teams which communicate well. Innovative teams:[83]

- collaborate
- have committed teamworkers
- tolerate diversity
- communicate well
- have practical support
- give positive encouragement to each other.

Integrated teams

In one integrated primary care nursing team, nurses formed a team and appointed a nominated leader who co-ordinated the work and resolved any overlaps or conflicts in relation to which particular members had various roles or responsibilities. The leader liaised with the GPs and practice manager over the delivery of care in line with the practice's objectives.[84]

A detailed study of integrated nursing teams yielded the following findings.[82]

Good points

- The team was highly structured, problem focused and goal orientated.
- Multiprofessional practices such as note-keeping, assessment, monitoring and evaluation were common.
- Team members were willing to be flexible about their roles.
- Being a team player was as important as being a member of a particular discipline.
- A learning culture was facilitated and supported by the heads of departments.

Not-so-good points

- Not all nurses were clear and confident about their roles.
- Problem-solving skills varied in the team.
- Although teaching between professionals was common, nurses seemed to be excluded from a teaching role.
- It was difficult to integrate a newcomer into the team because she had a different philosophy about teamworking.

Integrated teams may not be exclusive to nurses. One multidisciplinary integrated team attributed its success to a team member:

- being prepared to demonstrate their skills so that all team members could observe what each of the others was doing
- being clear about their role and contribution
- being flexible about working across role boundaries where necessary.

The benefits of this integrated teamworking were as follows:

- *for patients*: continuity, consistency, appropriate referrals, less ambiguity, holistic information and better problem solving
- *for team members*: professional development through the exchange of knowledge and skills.

Box 4.4:   The organisational factors that facilitate integrated teamwork[82]

An integrated team working in a rehabilitation unit attributed their cohesion to the following six organisational factors:

- working close together
- having a stable environment
- being able to predict what happens
- being a specialist team
- having supportive management structures
- having matching organisational policies.

You may not have all of these ingredients in the team in which you work. Cohesion was the essential ingredient in these studies for successful integrated teamwork – so focus on that first in your own work situation.

Teambuilding

When power is managed well, it can encourage security, support and trust with frank and open discussion and negotiation – all of which are part of *teambuilding*.[25]

Teambuilding starts from the top. Managers and senior clinicians should set good examples that encourage trust and respect from other colleagues. Without this, no organisation will be able to function to its full potential. This takes time, effort and consistency, but you will reap the rewards.

Teams may break down as a result of poor management, lack of guidance, poor communication and poor support. Games are often instigated by people who want to hang on to power, who may feel insecure or threatened by others. Power is a *bargaining chip* that people will try to grab, steal or manipulate. When power in any organisation is abused or mismanaged, the results will inevitably lead to a dysfunctional work environment. This can lead to the same problems that beset a dysfunctional family – it falls apart.

Unless the difficulties are acknowledged and the management is fully committed to the concept of teambuilding, attempts to improve the situation are likely to be a waste of time and resources. If managers are equivocal about teambuilding, and the staff who attend teambuilding activities are the least influential ones who can most easily be spared, the long-term result will be that nothing will change. Failed attempts to improve team relationships will simply reinforce the staff's cynicism.

Exercise 4.1:   How well is your team functioning?

Good teamwork does not just happen. Take time out as a team away from the workplace to review how you are working together. Everyone should have an equal chance to give their perspective on how the team is functioning.

Take the challenge below (from Chambers and Davies[25]).

There is good communication between colleagues at work.
Usually   *Seldom*   *Not at all*
There is good communication between managers and staff.
Usually   *Seldom*   *Not at all*
Team members' functions are clear.
Usually   *Seldom*   *Not at all*
Staff are proud to be working in your practice/unit.
Usually   *Seldom*   *Not at all*
Doctors/managers resolve staff problems.
Usually   *Seldom*   *Not at all*
Staff are treated with respect by doctors and managers.
Usually   *Seldom*   *Not at all*
There is a person-friendly culture at work.
Usually   *Seldom*   *Not at all*
There are opportunities for self-improvement for staff.
Usually   *Seldom*   *Not at all*
Positive feedback about performance is the norm at work.
Usually   *Seldom*   *Not at all*
Staff are well trained for the tasks that they are asked to do.
Usually   *Seldom*   *Not at all*
Team members' responsibilities are clear.
Usually   *Seldom*   *Not at all*
There is good leadership in your team.
Usually   *Seldom*   *Not at all*

Score: usually = 3, seldom = 1, not at all = 0.
Scores of between 27 and 36: you have a well-functioning team.
Scores of between 16 and 26: look at your weak areas and make plans for improvements.
Scores of 15 or below: as you have a long way to go, it may be best for you to consider using an external consultant to help to facilitate team development.

Defusing a stressful situation as a team

When defusing a particularly stressful situation at work it is necessary to be open, representative and fair. The recipe for handling stress in this way is to:

- establish an open forum for staff to air their grievances and worries in a 'safe' environment
- hold meetings regularly
- encourage everyone to have their say, and not allow one or two members of staff to dominate the meetings
- establish clear leadership in the team
- arrange for a skilled facilitator to advise your organisation if stress at work is threatening the stability or performance of the team, or send staff on external stress management courses if this is appropriate
- tackle difficult issues, and not allow problems to drift on, provoking stress.

Leading by example

The principles of self-leadership apply as much in the NHS as in any other field.

The essentials of self-leadership are as follows:

- awareness of self-limiting thoughts and emotional triggers
- clarity of vision
- direction
- motivation and enthusiasm
- flexibility of mind
- innovation
- coping with change
- working together co-operatively
- achieving to your maximum capability.

A team leader needs to have a vision for the team which they share with team members so that the vision guides their actions. They should know where they want the team to go and be clear about the team's philosophy and aims. The actions that the team takes should anticipate any future changes in working practices that are required to achieve the vision and aims, and prepare for those changes through recruitment, enhancing current skills of team members, introducing new systems and processes, etc.

Teams do better with a democratic leader than with an autocratic one. If you are the leader, you should be aiming to create a culture in which every member of the team feels valued for the work that they do, and knows that their views about the way in which the team functions and progresses will be respected and listened to.

A team leader should:[85]

- have a clear strategy for achieving their team's future goals and vision
- lead by example whenever possible
- learn to adapt to change and enable team members to adapt to change
- agree specific and realistic goals with clear deadlines
- be creative and innovative, absorbing the risks that these approaches incur
- create opportunities for inter-team and external collaboration and joint working
- be sensitive to the needs and expectations of team members
- provide opportunities for personal and professional development for team members in a fair and equitable way
- develop the forward planning ability and capacity to handle crises effectively
- promote the work of the team and its successes whenever possible, both within the team and to the outside world
- resolve interpersonal conflicts
- enthuse team members and continue to keep them motivated as a coherent team.

Time management[5]

A certain degree of time pressure is probably necessary for you to maintain your interest and momentum in getting a job done. However, too much pressure could tip you over your performance peak so that you are less efficient and your work suffers as you become less effective.

You have probably been conditioned by your training and work to feel that you must cope regardless of the time pressures. You may feel that patients must not suffer whatever the costs to you and your colleagues. However, there are limits to your tolerance, and if too much pressure is exerted in this way for too long, you may end up feeling burnt out and consider leaving your job. Therefore you must learn to control the demands on your time before any excessive pressures affect you and your performance adversely.

One of the commonest sources of stress for people working in the NHS is time pressure. The key to good time management is to:

- balance your work and leisure time
- prioritise the way in which you spend your time – do not allow yourself or others to waste it

- control interruptions
- include time for thinking, doing, meeting and learning in your working day
- allow sufficient time for the unexpected
- delegate work whenever it is appropriate, both at work and at home
- try only to accept delegated work if you have the necessary skills, time and experience, and arrange further training if necessary
- get on with essential tasks and not procrastinate
- be assertive – learn to say 'no' often enough, both to unnecessary work and to taking on other people's jobs and tasks
- make effective decisions and not look back
- put past mistakes behind you – do not ruminate over them
- review significant problems and learn to manage time better so as to avoid those problems in future – by making realistic action plans.

Many of these methods of time control depend on systems and processes in your workplace being reorganised. This is why time management has been included in the chapter describing what teams can do to beat stress at work.

Balance your work and leisure time successfully

One important way to reduce stress is to timetable enough free time during your day to allow yourself to have space for rest and relaxation to counteract the stresses and strains of your working life.

You and your colleagues should try to complete work activities within your normal working hours, so that you have enough time for non-work-related activities in your lives. If you do not allow sufficient time for leisure, you will not have the opportunity for personal growth outside work and will probably become stale. Every so often, you might set a target to learn or improve at something outside work, or take active measures to nurture your relationships with your partner, family and friends (e.g. by sharing a new hobby).

The best options are solutions that make regular time and space for yourself for fun, relaxation, hobbies and enjoying simple pleasures throughout your life as a *stress-proofing* measure. Don't suddenly try to adopt these methods to beat stress at one particular time in your working life, when you are already functioning below par. One effective way of monitoring whether you are managing to protect enough time for yourself is to keep a daily log of activities for a week or so.

Exercise 4.2: Keep a log of your daily activities for a week

Photocopy the daily log on page 75 and record all of your activities each day for a week, including an off-duty period if possible. Sort the activities into three separate columns as follows:

- *personal needs*, including shopping, sleeping, domestic chores, bodily needs, etc.
- *work*, including reading work-related books, reports and papers
- *leisure*, including sport, relaxation, reading, music, etc.

Work out totals for the types of activities for each day. Compare your daily recordings with the former Health Education Authority's recommendations for a healthy lifestyle by grouping your activities into the same categories:[86]

- 45–55% on personal needs
- 25–30% on work
- 20–25% on leisure.

When the work component increases above 25%, it is usually the leisure proportion of the day that is reduced.

After you have kept the log, review how your totals compare with the Health Education Authority's guidelines. Enter your totals below.

- *Personal needs*:
- *Work*:
- *Leisure*:

Can you note any trends or patterns of activities (e.g. staying at work late, catching up on paperwork at home, etc.) from your daily time logs?
Were you generally in control of the time spent on different activities in your days, or did events control you? *Yes, I was in control/No, events controlled me.*
For what proportion of your daily timetables were your activities fixed (e.g. management or case meetings or clinics)? How many hours are generally under your control each day where activities might be rescheduled differently?

- *Number of hours at work under your control*:
- *Number of hours outside work under your control*:

What were the biggest timewasters for you?

- *At work*:
- *Outside work*:

How much of your leisure time was spent doing what you wanted to do?
Were there any surprises arising from the daily time logs?

continued overleaf

Do you need to make changes in your life to create more protected time for yourself (and your family)? What do you intend to do and when?:

Intend to:	Start date:
1	
2	
3	
4	
5	

Prioritise your time

Prioritise your time – do not allow yourself or others to waste it. Be clear about your goals, in your work and home life, or leisure. The way in which you allot your time will look very different if your main goal is to be a great golfer, to learn a new skill such as advanced computing, or to spend as much time as possible with your family. Plan your goals in association with whoever else they affect, and if you have more than one goal make sure that your goals do not conflict with each other.

Once you have established your goals and set out your strategies to achieve them, you need to structure sufficient time around those priorities. Look back at the results of the week in which you logged your time spent on daily activities, and map out the activities and tasks that are essential at work and at home. Programme your priority activities in, either as a paper exercise or by thinking them through and resolving on a new schedule.

When an activity arises and you can choose whether or not to take it on, match it against your goals. If it takes you further away from your goals, then refuse to take it on, but if it brings you closer to achieving your goals, consider whether you have time to fit it in. Be firm with yourself, and do not agree to do it just because you like the person who is asking you and want to please them – guard against being distracted from the hurly-burly of work and diverted from your overall objectives.

Make sure that you spend your quality time doing the most important or complex jobs. It is too easy to focus on getting small unimportant tasks done,

DAILY LOG OF ACTIVITIES

Time spent on activities (to nearest quarter of an hour)					
Personal needs (shopping, washing, domestic chores, sleeping)		Work		Leisure	
Activity	Time spent	Activity	Time spent	Activity	Time spent
	Total for day:		Total for day:		Total for day:

and to put off tackling the large ones, which then hang over you and make you feel guilty about leaving them unattended.

A high-priority task has to be done, a medium-priority task may be delegated, and a low-priority task should only be done if you have no medium- or high-priority tasks waiting, or if you are feeling too jaded to tackle them.

Control interruptions

Interruptions are one of the biggest timewasters, especially if someone else could have handled the problem or taken the message, or no action was required. Even if an interruption is necessary, it may occur at the wrong time, wrecking your concentration or train of thought. Agree rules in your workplace with regard to who may be interrupted and when. Work out a system (and keep to it!) with your colleagues and manager at work for letting others know when you are not to be disturbed and are spending quality time on priority tasks, and when you are available to deal with the queries that have built up while you were occupied. Keep focused on your priorities and do not allow others to engage you in chat when you are intent on work. For example, your concentration may be continually distracted if other members of staff constantly invade the treatment room to fetch equipment while you are in the midst of treating patients. Or if you work in the community, you may feel frustrated and time pressured if you have to keep breaking off from your home visits and journeying back to base for briefing meetings that are held at inconvenient times, or when it was not necessary to deliver the briefing in person.

You could get into the habit of regarding minutes or hours as costed time. Think of how much some of the activities on which you spend time are worth, and whether different activities are of equal worth.

Include sufficient time for thinking, doing, meeting, developing and learning

You need to be fresh and creative in order to stay on top of the demands that are made on you as a health professional and to remain productive. You can only manage this in the longer term if you have the right mix of stimulating work, personal and professional development and networking regularly timetabled into your daily schedule. Persistent overwork will be counterproductive, and it will be a negative stress which may lead to your becoming less effective.

You will achieve more in designated sessions of quiet uninterrupted periods than in a longer allotment of time that is broken up by various activities. This is the time for planning, writing reports or analysing progress.

Try to allocate at least 10% of your time to dealing with unexpected tasks. Looking after patients invariably means that you will have unexpected work to do. In the unlikely event that everything goes smoothly and you do not need the extra time, it will be a bonus to have that additional space in which to catch up on the backlog of paperwork, or simply spend a little more time talking to patients or colleagues.

Your own preference for thinking time will depend on your personality. Extroverts will be revitalised by brainstorming and discussions with a group of others, while those who are more introverted will prefer protected space in which to reflect and read. Whichever you prefer, make sure that you get enough protected space to replenish your creativity and enthusiasm. Some enjoy meeting with local groups of like-minded colleagues that are a mix of support, education and social activities. Many nurses are joining in clinical supervision groups. Learning Sets are also springing up that offer development and support to small groups of peers or others from different health disciplines. You might benefit from finding a buddy who is in similar circumstances to you, in order to listen to each other and exchange ideas and support through regular meetings.

Sometimes groups of colleagues need external facilitation so that people do not fall into the trap of moaning, complaining or competing with regard to who has the most difficult time or most stress.

Delegate whatever and however you can

If you are in a position to delegate work and responsibilities, decide what only *you* can do, and delegate as much of the rest as possible to others. It is important to minimise duplication so that work and initiatives are co-ordinated over different disciplines as much as possible (e.g. so that social workers, district nurses and practice nurses are not doing similar work with the same patients in parallel or in duplicate).

If you are more often on the receiving end of delegated work, try to make sure that you understand what is required, and that you have the time, skills and experience necessary before agreeing or acquiescing to taking on the new work. There is great potential for time wasting if you try to carry out delegated work when you do not know what is required or how to set about doing it. If you do not have the time or skills necessary for the additional work, try to negotiate how you will get the training and when you will do the work in your most assertive manner.

You should consider delegation not just at work, but also at home. If you find it difficult to relinquish control, and like to be seen as achieving in all spheres of your life (super-nurse, super-homemaker, super-parent, super-spouse, etc.) you may need convincing that it is perfectly acceptable to minimise time spent on the chores at home when you are so busy at work. If you can afford it, employing domestic or gardening help is one of the most effective ways of instantly obtaining more quality time at home. If you cannot afford it, you will have to recruit all of the family to help, using a fair rota system, rather than trying to do most of the chores yourself.

Prioritise and delegate.

Don't procrastinate: get on with essential tasks

So what are you waiting for? Distasteful or complicated tasks are the ones that people procrastinate over. However, if it is an essential or important task, you will have to do it some time, and you will only feel guilty if you put it off. If you procrastinate too long the job will be even more difficult, as you will forget your previous ideas or what the instructions were. If you train yourself to do the least wanted task first, you can reward yourself with a more pleasing job or even free time.

Wait until you have time to complete a stage or the whole of a job. Don't pick up a piece of paper and half read it, decide that it is too difficult to tackle or that you do not have enough time and then put it down again. You will have wasted that time deciding to put off the job. And if you are in this procrastinating state of mind, you may welcome unnecessary interruptions and thus compound the time wasting further. Try to get yourself geared up for the job and launch into it.

Control your work flow

As well as using the control techniques described above, you should review the flow of your work to match your capacity. You are more likely to be most productive with a steady flow of work rather than arranging your day as a pressure/slack/pressure sandwich. If you work in a general practice, the surgery times may mean that there is 'dead time' in the middle of the day when you are less productive because the pressure is off and you waste time by taking longer to do small tasks, only to find that you invariably finish work late after a pressured evening surgery. If that is the case, you will have to find ways as a practice to change the work flow in the system to suit you better (e.g. by changing booking times, or moving evening meetings to earlier slots in the day, etc.). If you work in a hospital setting, you might find that the work flow is uneven if you work in outpatient clinics where the ambulance transport suddenly delivers shoals of patients to the clinics, or when a series of emergencies are admitted to the wards. Again you will have to organise yourselves as a team to make sure that as many non-urgent jobs as possible are done in quieter periods in order to keep up a steady work flow.

Concentrate on one task at a time. Complete it and then either move on to another job or take a short break to refresh yourself and clear your mind ready to start again. Don't move from one task to another, or you will waste effort, as you will have to start thinking about the topic all over again each time you take it up.

If you are swamped by work you will be less efficient and more forgetful, which may create even more time pressure if you have to put right the problem caused by your forgetting something or missing an appointment. You are likely to be more efficient if you group small similar tasks together (e.g. returning telephone calls). Always have one or two small jobs put by, or carry them with you, so that if you are kept waiting you can get on with those tasks and not waste time. Maintain control of your paperwork. Do not allow it to build up so that you feel overwhelmed, or you will put off tackling it at all, or work more slowly because the enormity of the task depresses you.

Limit the amount of time that you spend on the telephone. If you measure how long you talk for the next few times you are on the phone, you will probably be surprised by how many minutes the calls last for. Tape a few telephone calls and listen to yourself – you may find that much of the time is spent on pleasantries or repeating what you have already said.

Be assertive: say 'no' to unnecessary work or other people's jobs and tasks

The greatest challenge is to be assertive with yourself so that you do not agree to take on additional tasks that are not essential for you to undertake, or that fall outside your own priority areas. If you are not careful, you may find that you are so busy helping others that you do not get your own work done.

Make effective decisions

Be decisive and finish the jobs in hand. Gather information about a problem or choice, weigh up the pros and cons, and then make a decision. Once you have made that decision, look forward and make plans for the future – don't look backwards and frame regrets.

Some tips on making effective decisions are listed below.

- There are always other options – find out what they are.
- Gather ideas and evidence from other people or a range of sources – do not be confined to just those options that you already know about.
- Base your analyses and decisions on reliable objective evidence or observations, and not on 'guesstimates'.
- Think through the implications of a decision by considering the possible consequences before choosing which options to take.
- Information is about feelings as well as facts – what the situation really is and how people feel about it.
- Your personality and beliefs will affect your decision-making process.
- Don't accept other people's perceptions of reality – look and think for yourself.
- Be honest with yourself and others, and keep your integrity. The best decisions are based on truth, not on illusions.
- Effective decisions are based on reality, not on hope.
- Probing questions help to distinguish between illusion and reality.
- Simple decisions are usually best, and are often obvious in retrospect.
- Fear gets in the way of making realistic assessments of the options.
- Don't make decisions because you are frightened of something, but because you are enthusiastic about the expected outcomes.

The more aware you are of your own character, the better you will understand the way in which you make decisions. How you feel about the way in which you make a decision often forecasts the results. If you feel good about a decision, the outcome is usually a success.

Looking after the welfare of other team members

Employers should make sure that the job plans of each member of the team identify time for any managerial responsibilities and their professional development. This is all part of the Duty of Care of Employers.

There should be sufficient administrative and technological support for health professionals in carrying out their roles. Every health professional will not be able to carry out every aspect of their role all of the time with the staffing levels of today's NHS. Individual team members will need help in order to prioritise and delegate their workload.

Someone should be responsible for overseeing workload, and in a position to take appropriate action if the volume or intensity is compromising the quality of patient care, opportunities and time for individuals' professional development, or a reasonable balance between work and home life.

Good practice in recruitment and selection of new staff is an important aspect of creating and maintaining a happy and flourishing team. Consider each time whether you are about to appoint the right employee to the right job – don't make do and hope for the best. Re-advertise rather than make a dubious appointment. Similarly, staff members should be promoted to the right job at the right time, and any induction, training and support that they will need for the role and responsibilities of their new post will have to be anticipated.

Undertaking a risk assessment of work-related stress in your workplace[23]

If you are going to create a relatively stress-free working environment for staff in your workplace, you need to assess the degree of stress and determine the factors that are provoking it at present, predict the stressors that will occur from time to time, and review the systems that you have in place for controlling and minimising stressors. Don't rely on people's self-reports, but instead undertake a risk assessment in a systematic manner. You might set up a steering group of representatives from your team to oversee the risk assessment project and ensure that everyone's views are considered. Your findings will be a balance of the negative aspects of work and working conditions and the positive measures taken to control stress-related problems and support employees and other colleagues.[87]

Risk assessment is a six-stage process.

1   Identify hazards – stressors which exist in relation to work and working conditions – and assess the degree of exposure of the various team members to those hazards.

2   Assess the harm. Is there evidence from sickness absence? Are there detrimental effects of stress on individuals or on the organisation as a whole?
3   Identify the likely risk factors. Are certain individuals more at risk?
4   Describe the underlying mechanisms. What is the link between the presumed stressor and the effects of provoking stress in individuals, or the detrimental effects on the organisation as a whole?
5   Audit the existing methods for controlling stress-provoking factors and the effectiveness of support systems.
6   Recommend ways to minimise work stress, taking the existing methods for controlling stress-provoking factors and supporting staff into account.

Work with everyone to identify significant or non-trivial sources of stress related to work and working conditions. As far as possible, look for objective evidence of the sources of stress and the effects on individuals or work done. Try to work at a level of detail which can inform any activities to minimise stress or reduce the risks of provoking stress.

Preventing stress at work after your risk assessment

You might address the results of your risk assessment by reducing the risks of stress at work in the following ways.

1   *Primary prevention*: promoting the well-being of individual members of your team and forestalling their exposure to stress. Primary interventions are those that aim to eliminate or at least modify the occurrence of work-based stressors in the first instance, and they therefore occur at the organisational level.
2   *Secondary prevention*: early diagnosis of stresses that arise and prompt action in order to reduce the prevalence of stress in team members. These interventions help staff to develop their physical and psychological resources for limiting the damaging effects of stress when it does occur.
3   *Tertiary prevention*: helping to alleviate the effects of stress on individual team members. Tertiary interventions rehabilitate individuals who have succumbed to the negative effects of stress.[15]

Secondary and tertiary interventions are the predominant approach taken by organisations that are tackling stress management. Thus programmes tend to be run for individuals rather than for workplace teams or organisations as a whole. In improving employees' skills with regard to managing or resisting stress, this worker-orientated approach does not prevent the occurrence of stress. Prevention requires the meaningful involvement of the organisation in identifying and modifying workplace stressors.

Box 4.5:   Example of a risk assessment and subsequent risk reduction in the customer contact centre of a large utility firm[23]

This organisation has been chosen as an example for drawing out general lessons for a healthcare workplace because the essence of the organisation described here is about customer care.

The initial risk assessment was undertaken because the organisation had ambitious plans for change, staff reported low levels of job satisfaction and many wanted to leave, and staff absence rates due to sickness were moderate to high. There were also many problems relating to the design and management of work within the organisation.

The risk assessment revealed the following:

- unrealistic performance targets
- a lack of praise and recognition
- poor communication with senior management
- slow movement of information around the organisation
- having to deal with multiple tasks of equal importance
- lack of support from and poor availability of line managers
- lack of time to complete tasks
- inadequate time for breaks during the day.

(Do you notice the similarities between the above description and many NHS workplaces?)

The steering group overseeing the risk assessment produced the following extensive package of interventions targeted at the identified risk factors, the stressors and their underlying pathologies.

The interventions for reducing the risks of work-related stress included the following:

- changes in the management of performance targets
- the instigation of more regular, structured and purposeful team meetings
- measures to improve organisational communication
- the introduction of new training initiatives
- the introduction of quality monitoring
- the introduction of 'best practice' guidelines for working procedures
- a review and updating of staffing levels to meet increased public demand
- formal break-taking arrangements
- changes in IT systems and the introduction of new systems.

One year later, the results of the planned risk reduction were evaluated. Although some problems remained, there were many positive findings.

- There was a high level of awareness of the interventions (listed above).
- Staff reported that many of the interventions had improved their work.
- There was a drop in the number of stressors and risks reported by staff compared with the previous year.
- There was evidence of greater well-being among those who indicated that the interventions had improved their work and working conditions.
- Sickness absence rates were reduced and remained steady at around 5%.

Exercise 4.3:   Undertake a risk assessment of stress in your workplace

Date ....

Is there a 'hazard' that is provoking stress in the working environment, or affecting the capability of the staff?	How can this be avoided or minimised?	Is the risk adequately controlled? (Yes/No)	Further action needed

Conclusion to risk assessment exercise

1   What 'hazards' have you identified?
2   Do you and others in your team know how to avoid, minimise or eliminate those hazards? If not, include these topics in your personal development plan or workplace-based learning plan.
3   What is your action plan for your risk reduction programme? Be specific – give details of objectives, method, expected outcomes and timetable.

Constructing a stress management policy for your workplace

Is there a policy for stress management in your workplace or practice? If there is, is it written down and how does it compare with the checklist below? If there is not, you could construct a policy using the checklist below as an *aide-mémoire*. The policy should:

- be written down
- outline good management practices (e.g. good communication, positive work culture, promotion of job satisfaction, good leadership, well-organised systems, etc.) to minimise stress arising from the way in which the organisation runs
- be familiar to all staff
- have a designated date for review
- have a system for staff to offer feedback on how the policy is working in practice
- name the person who is responsible for monitoring the procedures and standards described in the policy
- describe the steps for a preceding risk assessment of work-related stress
- contain procedures to identify and take action on stress *hot spots* within the workplace or practice
- be clear as to who will take action and when if stress levels become too high
- specify to whom staff should take problems which cause them stress or distress
- include a routine system for post-traumatic stress counselling or discussion after a very stressful event has occurred at work
- describe sources of inter-practice and external support that are available to staff
- state how staff sickness absence is monitored and handled
- include a forum within the practice where staff can discuss problems that cause stress in a 'safe' environment (i.e. one which is non-judgemental and confidential)
- cover pre-employment procedures designed to select candidates who will fit into the work team, and who are well matched to the post and team
- describe arrangements for the rehabilitation of staff who are sick
- include the procedure for obtaining an independent opinion if the management is in conflict with a member of staff about whether they are too sick or stressed to be able to work.

Using clinical governance to reduce the levels of stress in your workplace

Clinical governance underpins professional and service development. Clinical governance is 'doing anything and everything required to maximise quality'.[88] It is about finding ways to implement care that works in an environment in which clinical effectiveness can flourish.

We should be moving towards team-based learning that includes everyone, whether they are a doctor, nurse, therapist or manager, or provide non-clinical support. Clinical governance will underpin both individual and team-based personal and professional development plans.

The quality of the workforce dictates the quality of the healthcare that they deliver. An effective workforce is one in which individuals are competent to carry out their current roles and responsibilities, and their training anticipates new models of service delivery. Achieving this requires sufficient resources and the right learning environment throughout the health service. The future is in multidisciplinary learning as work-based teams, addressing topics that are relevant to the needs of the local population, with clinicians and managers working closely together to put that learning into action.

Clinical governance underpins this way of working and accounting for the following:

*   sustaining quality improvements
*   minimising inequalities in the health of different subgroups of the patient population
*   reducing variations in healthcare services
*   defining standards
*   demonstrating achievements.

The emphasis is on education and training programmes being relevant to service needs, whether at organisational or individual levels. 'Continuing professional development programmes need to meet both the learning needs of individual health professionals to inspire public confidence in their skills ... and the wider service development needs of the NHS.'[89] Continuing professional development is not just about what you *want* to do, but also what you *need* to do.

Lifelong learning and continuing professional development are integral to the concept of clinical governance. Everyone should have learning goals that are relevant to service development.

Build up your stress-assessing and stress-reducing activities into a clinical governance plan for your practice or workplace. Think laterally using the 14 different components of clinical governance described on page 90 as a checklist. The example below has been included to help to guide you in your own plan. It tackles supporting staff in undergoing a change in the NHS, through learning practical self-management skills to cope with work-based pressures in order to enhance their performance and improve the quality of care that they provide.

It is important to target time and resources to consolidate best practice in the areas of clinical governance, as well as for training and education. The aim is to have an NHS workforce with the right combination of skills working within an efficient organisation in order to deliver effective, modern, patient-centred services. This means staff who are multi-skilled and personally effective.

An example of a clinical governance plan for reducing stress levels in a practice or other NHS workplace

It may be that a manager or clinical lead for clinical governance organises everyone to agree and compose the plan, and that this individual is in charge of implementing it.

Improving the workforce through staff support and development in a facilitatory organisational culture[90,91]

How was the focus of the clinical governance plan chosen?
The importance of the issue has been highlighted in a number of Government documents and initiatives (e.g. NHS Modernisation Agenda, the Health at Work Programme, Duty of Care of Employers). Staff are seen as central to the effectiveness of the organisation. The chief executive/lead manager might have suggested the need for the plan, backed by a previous survey of staff or team members that demonstrates the need.

Links with clinical governance agenda:

• improving quality
• the learning culture
• well-managed resources and services
• health gain
• accountability and performance.

Justify why the topic is a priority
A trust or practice priority? A district priority? A national priority?
At all three levels this topic is a priority. The expectations that are placed on services are increasing, and there is a mismatch between resources and demands. In view of the huge costs to the service of sickness absence, trained people leaving the profession, litigation, advertising, recruiting and retraining, there is an urgent need to focus on the individual within the work environment of the health service. If we can support staff to manage themselves and their

work-based pressure more effectively, their motivation, well-being and job satisfaction are likely to increase. This will have a direct spin-off in terms of both the quality of the work that they do and the teams of which they are a part.

Who will be included in the clinical governance plan?

Give posts and names of doctors, nurses, therapists, managers, non-clinical staff, others from outside the practice, and patients

All staff should be included. The plan should initially be focused on specific groups or a team, and in large services through a cascade process of internal training using the course structure.

Who will collect the baseline information and how?

External consultants will collect information on work pressures and day-to-day concerns that affect performance and work productivity. There will be a formal assessment of staff using a scale of perceived work stress.[92,93]

Where are you now?

- Survey of staff views will give insight into concerns that they have (*see* below).
- External consultant's findings (*see* above).
- General levels and patterns of employee sickness absence.
- Patients' views, looking at levels of complaints about the health services and care that we provide. Use feedback from local community forums (e.g. looking at healthy and safe communities) or patients' advisory and liaison services (PALS) within the hospital or trust.

What information will you obtain about individuals' learning wishes and needs?

How will you obtain this and who will do it? Self-completion checklists, discussion, appraisal, feedback?

Staff will complete anonymised forms outlining areas of pressure in their day-to-day working lives and their concerns. These aspects will be collated and questionnaires sent out to confirm the areas under consideration for inclusion in the training programme for the team (e.g. time spent on managing stress, creating an organisational vision, teambuilding, looking at leadership, etc.). Evaluation and feedback forms will be reviewed after the workshops attended by staff.

There will be continuing consultation with staff at all levels, and production of a report outlining recommendations and opportunities for sustaining the work-related stress reduction programme within the organisation (e.g. training staff within the setting to continue the work, 'booster' workshops, use of materials, etc.).

What are the service development and associated learning needs of the practice, hospital or trust and how do they match the needs of individuals?
Best practice includes making preventative training, counselling and stress management services available to staff, as well as organisational consultancy and individual case work.

As a preventative process, the training of staff in stress management should focus on participants' attitudes, linking their knowledge and practice in order to hone the underlying skills to enable greater empowerment. This should promote the maintenance of well-being both for staff themselves and for others, rather than emphasising the treatment of ill health. Awareness of communication issues and the role of interrelationship skills affecting health outcomes will also feature.

How will you prioritise everyone's needs in a fair and open way?
Agree the structure needed to implement the training programme throughout the organisation so that it is accessible for everyone and individualised for particular staff groups with special needs. The materials that are employed should allow staff to use reflective practice and self-directed learning to maintain the process after they have attended the course.

What patient or public input is there into the plan?
Quality assurance is built into this plan by gathering patients' views about the services received when establishing the baseline and how to proceed (*see* above).

Action plan
June: A preliminary staff survey is undertaken in parallel with the external consultant's review.
August: An organisational change programme examining quality assurance is under way.
The views of participants and the hospital or trust board are solicited.
There is agreement to run a staff support and development programme.
October onwards: Initial workshops are run alongside the organisational change programme.
December onwards: Follow-up workshops start to run.
March: Feedback and evaluations are collated.
April: Data are analysed in preparation of the report.
May: A framework is presented to the senior partner or manager of the practice/department, or the chief executive, directors and board for future 'in-house training' to expand the programme, together with a planned programme for organisational change.
June onwards: There is continued evaluation and revision, maintenance and sustaining of the project in order to improve quality and staff working climate

or environment from all perspectives – those of the staff, management and patients.

How might you integrate the 14 components of clinical governance into your clinical governance plan?

Establishing a learning culture: hold an in-house educational session on controlling stress for team members.

Managing resources and services: control key sources of stress such as reducing the impact of patients needing to be seen on the same day as 'urgent' cases, or reducing interruptions.

Establishing a research and development culture: conduct a survey to identify sources of stress, or compare the levels of demand before and after the introduction of an intervention.

Reliable and accurate data: team members learn to become more competent at operating the computer.

Evidence-based practice and policy: updating clinicians' knowledge of the evidence for best practice for common clinical conditions may relieve feelings of guilt and uncertainty that were causing stress, and reduce the potential for making mistakes.

Confidentiality: preserve the confidentiality of team members if they are patients at the practice or hospital trust.

Health gain: reducing individuals' stress levels will result in less physical symptoms of stress as well as associated medication such as analgesics, indigestion remedies, etc.

Coherent team: good communication between team members should reduce stress for all – perhaps by producing and distributing a news-sheet when changes are expected.

Audit and evaluation: audit will be part of the learning needs or risk assessment to identify the sources and effects of stress, and the (hopefully) beneficial effects of any intervention will be evaluated.

Meaningful involvement of patients and the public: seeking patients' views (e.g. through focus groups) might help to improve access so that, with more appropriate booking of patients, staff are not under such a great time pressure when patients consult.

Health promotion: promote stress reduction for staff (e.g. the mental strategies described in Chapter 3).

Risk management: using a risk assessment, reduction and management approach for the personal safety of staff should identify, avoid or minimise risk factors which threaten their safety and give rise to stress.

Accountability and performance: being under too much stress for too long will inevitably make staff less effective. This should be reversible with good stress management.

Core requirements: staff are more likely to adopt new approaches that are more cost-effective if they are less stressed and more willing to embrace change.

5

Beating stress at work in the NHS: through personal development planning

Your personal development plan will allow you to demonstrate your fitness to practise or manage stress, whether you are a doctor, nurse, therapist or manager. It will form a significant part of your continuing professional development portfolio, ready for any appraisal or professional review.

You will need to set aside enough time to shape and justify your learning plan. The more time you invest in drawing up your plan and the programme of learning, the more likely it is that you will focus your learning effectively.

The main task is to capture what you have learned in a way that suits you, so that you can look back at what you have done and:

- reflect on it at a later date, in order to learn more, make changes as a result, and identify further needs
- demonstrate to others that you are fit to practise or work – through what you have done, what you have learned and what changes you have made as a result, the standards of work you have achieved and are maintaining, and how you monitor your performance at work
- use it to show how your personal learning fits in with the practice or trust's business plan, and the practice or workplace personal and professional development plans.

Draw up your personal development plan

You should integrate your personal development plan with your colleagues' plans. Your workplace personal and professional development plan should cater for everyone who works in the team. Clinical governance principles will balance the development needs of the population, your practice or department, hospital or trust, and your individual personal development plan.

If you are working on a project that involves change for other people as well as for yourself, it is better to work together towards a common goal and co-ordinate multiprofessional learning across traditional boundaries.

If you work in a number of different roles or posts, reflect on the boundaries between your roles so that you are able to focus your learning to meet your needs in one role to benefit others.

The worked example on pages 99–103 demonstrates how you might set about preparing and undertaking your own programme based on *stress management.*

Modify the worked example on stress management to match your own ideas and circumstances. You might find that a personal development plan on one topic is all that you can manage in the course of one year, especially if you widen your programme around the various components of clinical governance that you incorporate into your plan. For instance, considering the evidence base with regard to 'stress management' might lead you to search for and apply the evidence in relation to various psychological and alternative therapies for patients. If you decide that the priorities for you to learn about include generalisable topics such as 'effective teamworking', 'good communication systems' or 'leadership', then you can see that such a personal development plan will feed into all of the areas of your professional life and might be as much as you could cope with in one year.

The following template should help you to prepare your own plan. Photocopy the pages – and get on with it! Demonstrate what you have achieved and keep a learning record.

Template for your personal development plan

What topic have you chosen?

Who chose it?

Justify why this topic is a priority:

a personal or professional priority?

a workplace priority?

a national priority?

continued opposite

Who will be included in your personal development plan? (Anyone other than you? Colleagues, others from outside the practice/department, patients?)

What baseline information will you collect and how? How will you identify your learning needs? (How will you obtain this information and who will do it? Self-completion checklists, discussion, appraisal, audit, patient feedback?)

What are the learning needs of the practice/department and how do they match your needs?

Is there any patient or public input to your personal development plan?

Aims of your personal development plan arising from the preliminary data-gathering exercise:

How might you integrate the 14 components of clinical governance into your personal development plan focusing on the topic of ....?

As you work through this clinical governance checklist, identify what learning needs you have to match the service needs you identify, and shape your action learning plan accordingly. These needs might include learning more about time management, communication and negotiation to enable you to function more effectively within the team.

Establishing a learning culture:

continued overleaf

Managing resources and services:

Establishing a research and development culture:

Reliable and accurate data:

Evidence-based practice and policy:

Confidentiality:

Health gain:

Coherent team:

Audit and evaluation:

Meaningful involvement of patients and the public:

Health promotion:

Risk management:

Accountability and performance:

Core requirements:

continued opposite

Action learning plan (include timetabled action and expected outcomes)

How does your personal development plan tie in with other strategic plans?

What additional resources will you require to execute your plan and from where do you hope to obtain them? (Will you have to pay any course fees? Will you be able to organise any protected time for learning in working hours?)

continued overleaf

How will you evaluate your personal development plan?

How will you know when you have achieved your objectives? (How will you measure success?)

How will you disseminate the learning from your plan to the rest of the team and patients? How will you sustain your new-found knowledge or skills?

How will you handle new learning requirements as they crop up?

Record of your learning activities

Enter activity, time taken, when undertaken, etc.

	Activity 1	Activity 2	Activity 3	Activity 4
In-house formal learning				
External courses				
Informal and personal				
Qualifications and/or experience gained				

Escalating workload.

Worked example of a personal development plan, focused on stress management from a nurse's perspective

Justify why the topic of stress management is a priority:

(i)   *A personal or professional priority?* After working as a nurse for 20 years, I realise that my job satisfaction is being whittled away by the stresses I am experiencing at work from the many demands that are made on me. I think that the effects of this stress are starting to threaten the quality of my day-to-day work.

(ii)   *A workplace priority?* A nurse who is under stress affects all members of the team. This may be because I, as a stressed nurse, create more work for others if my performance is below par (e.g. when I am forgetful or make mistakes). Being stressed may mean that I am reluctant to change from my routine.

(iii)   *A national priority?* The Government is emphasising the importance of good human resource management in the quality and well-being of the NHS workforce.

Who will be included in my personal development plan?

Although my personal development plan is focused on my needs, I cannot 'beat' stress without significant changes in the organisation of the practice. Therefore I will invite others to join in my initiative as it evolves, either learning to control stress for themselves, or becoming involved in reorganising the practice systems that create stress. The following could be included:

- doctors
- manager
- other nurses
- reception staff
- secretary
- my partner and family at home.

What baseline information will I collect?

The causes and effects of stress on me both at work and outside work.

How will I identify my learning needs?

- Audit of my everyday practice (e.g. significant event audits of several unexpected demands, such as extra patients, interruptions – whatever crops up over a couple of days).

- Observation of my practice by me personally using a stress log diary and self-assessment scores of perceived stress, and by informal comments from others.
- Observation of stressors in my life outside work by me personally using a stress log diary, and by informal comments from others.
- Comparing the methods of stress management that I know about with the list of possibilities given in a manual on stress management.
- Group discussion in a team meeting where the general topic of 'stress at work' is debated. I should learn more about the causes of stress for me by listening to what others find stressful and hearing more about their concerns and feelings.

What are the learning needs for others in my team and how do they match my needs?

If I learn to control some of the stresses on me, this should have additional benefits for others in the team, as I should be easier to work with, more efficient and a better communicator.

I shall have to take care that my suggestions for improving the systems and procedures at work reduce stress levels for everyone whenever possible. If I simply control stress on me by redirecting demands on others who do not have the time or inclination to absorb those demands, then I will be implementing my personal development plan at the expense of the overall good of the team, which is untenable.

Is there any patient or public input to my plan?

I shall use any complaints or informal feedback from patients if it is relevant to me, and that information might form the basis for a significant event audit. Unsolicited patient feedback might identify pressures at work that were previously unknown to me, or make me think about the causes or effects of stress for me, from which I might learn (e.g. remarks about punctuality, problems with regard to obtaining help or advice).

Aims of my personal development plan arising from the preliminary data-gathering exercise

These are to reduce stress at work by:

- identifying three significant sources of stress for me at work that are within my ability to control either as an individual or working with others in the team
- learning how to recognise causes of stress and their effects on me
- learning more about methods of stress management that are appropriate for the stressors I have identified, and how to apply them
- learning how it might be possible to improve systems and procedures at work, and how to involve others in the team in such reorganisation.

Action plan

Who is involved? Myself and anyone else in the team or associated with it with whom I work.

Timetabled action: Start date ...

By 3 months: preliminary data gathering completed and any other individuals involved in initiative identified.

• Is there a protocol at work for managing stress?
• Map expertise in the team (e.g. community psychiatric nurse, practice nurse with counselling skills); list other providers of help (e.g. Royal College of Nursing stress counselling service).
• Baseline information about sources of stress from completed stress log.

By 4 months: review current performance.

• Audits of actual performance according to pre-agreed criteria (e.g. numbers of interruptions while consulting in surgery or clinic; numbers of 'extra' patients seen in addition to booked surgeries/clinics).
• Compare performance with one or more of the 14 components of clinical governance described on page 90.

By 5 months: identify solutions and associated training needs.

• Learn new skills – in assertiveness, time management and delegation.
• Write or revise the protocol on stress management to include health surveillance and monitoring sources of stress at work.
• Clarify my roles at work – be more definite so that I know what my responsibilities are and will not feel guilty when others do not fulfil their duties.
• Apply the protocol for stress management, identify gaps, and propose changes to others at team meeting.
• Attend external courses or in-house training as appropriate.
• Visit another practice or directorate to see how they have combated their stressors.

By 10 months: make changes.

• Feed back information to the team about what is needed to reduce stress for me – and the others – prior to making changes (e.g. set up more opportunities for mutual support).
• Improve efficiency of the organisation from the perspectives of patients and staff.
• Produce a news-sheet once every 3 months describing any changes in the protocol or in people's roles and responsibilities.
• Arrange training for other nurses with whom I am sharing chronic disease management.

- Find a 'buddy' from outside my team with whom to discuss progress with our personal development plans.
- Re-register with a GP in whom I have complete trust.

Expected outcomes: more effective control of sources of stress; more efficient organisation at work; better teamwork, including communication and delegation; more effective performance at work; more willing to consider and implement change.

How does my learning plan tie in with other strategic plans?
It will tie in with the practice's or trust's development plan and with the NHS as a whole.

What additional resources will I require to execute my plan and from where do I hope to obtain them?
I will ask my manager to sponsor the costs of obtaining relaxation tapes for patients, which I shall use, too. I would expect to be able to fit attendance at a stress management course into my working day, and to pay any course fee myself, unless there is a bursary of some kind to cover my costs.

How will I evaluate my learning plan?
I shall use similar methods to those which I used to identify my learning needs as given earlier – keeping other stress logs of the pressures I perceive both at work and outside work, and re-auditing interruptions and the booking times after we have made changes and improved the practice organisation. I shall discuss with my 'buddy' how he or she thinks I am progressing with my personal development plan.

How will I know when I have achieved my objectives?
I shall re-audit and monitor my stress levels through a record log as described above, 12 months later. Then I shall determine whether I am using more effective coping methods to minimise any sources of stress that I have not been able to eliminate.

How will I disseminate the learning from my plan to the rest of the team and patients? How will I sustain my new-found knowledge or skills?
I shall share what I have learned at the peer support meeting that I will set up for other team members. I will encourage others to adopt 'health at work' for our joint personal and professional development plan, or at least for it to be the topic of an educational meeting for all of the team. I shall write an article for the nursing press on effective stress management in primary care!

Record of my learning about stress management

	Activity 1 – dealing with stress at work	Activity 2 – time management	Activity 3 – increasing support to beat stress	Activity 4 – identifying stressors and sources of pressure
In-house formal learning	Community psychiatric nurse ran a one-hour session on dealing with post-traumatic stress, after a member of staff died in a road accident		Organised first one-hour meeting at lunchtime to discuss setting up a regular support forum – facilitated by local lay counsellor	
External courses	One-day course at nearby postgraduate centre, small group learning – included several stress management methods	Learned about time management at same one-day course as Activity 1	Learned about support from same one-day course as Activity 1	
Informal and personal	Chat with staff over coffee, in corridors, etc.	Spent two hours peer assessing other practice or directorate as part of nurse training activities. Gained new ideas on time management from their practice manager	Read up on the topic from good manual on stress management. Did some of the interactive exercises	Fed audit results back to colleagues, manager and other staff at team meeting. Led discussion on what we will do about the problem areas (action plan to be submitted). Interesting discussion afterwards
Qualifications and/or experience gained?	Certificate for one-day course	Experience gained from comparing my practice (or directorate) with the other practice (or directorate)		

6

Beating stress at work in the NHS: make a logical plan to reduce stress in your working life

Advantages of a logical framework

The logical framework has been used for project planning for decades.[94] Development agencies have adopted the approach for planning and monitoring overseas programmes. Recently it has been used by the health service for planning and evaluating health action zone projects.[95,96]

You could regard reducing and managing the stresses and pressures in your life as a project, and use the logical framework (log frame) to think out your goals. This approach will force you to consider the assumptions you are making in setting out your action plan. You will be able to monitor your progress and pre-empt obstacles to your plans. The log frame is an aid to thinking rather than a series of procedures to which you should slavishly adhere. The framework will help you to concentrate on the operational aspects of your stress-managing 'project' – and who is doing what to whom, when, why and how.[94]

Thus we are adapting the log-frame approach so that you can use it to help you to undertake your personal project – to minimise stress for you at work in the NHS.

Why have your good resolutions to reduce stress or improve your life failed in the past? Is it because implementing your resolution was a much more complex matter than simply making the resolution? Other factors may have intruded that you had not foreseen. Your will-power might not have been sufficient, you might not have had the skills, time or money for your promised new way of life, or you may have mistakenly assumed that others would support you.

So think of using a project management approach to take control of your life – your activities, achievements, purpose and goals. The log-frame approach handles the complex nature of making and undertaking an action plan to reduce stress across all the dimensions of your life. The framework encourages you to set specific goals. It helps you to analyse your weaknesses and guides you in considering the assumptions that you are making – in the details of your plan of action or in pursuing your goals. This approach helps you to realise the interactions between what you can do for yourself and the external factors that either enhance or hinder your plans. The log frame helps you to set out realistic milestones and decide in advance how you will monitor your progress. It helps you to:

- organise your thinking
- relate your planned activities to the results that you can expect
- set performance indicators for yourself
- allocate responsibilities for yourself and others – at home, and within your practice or organisation.

The structure of the log frame consists of a 4×4 matrix. The rows represent the project objectives and the means of achieving them (vertical logic), and the columns indicate how you can verify that you have achieved your objectives (horizontal logic) and the assumptions that you are making.

The vertical logic

- *Step 1*. Define your overall *goal* – the reason for you undertaking the 'project'. This is the ultimate objective of your stress management programme. Phrase this in your own words. An example might be *to minimise stress in my working life*.
- *Step 2*. Define the *purpose* of the 'project'. The purpose is why you are proposing to carry out the project – what it will achieve once it is completed within your timescale, and what impact you hope to make. It is the motivation behind the outputs of the project (*see* Step 3). An example might be *to implement new stress management systems and programme*. It keeps the project more streamlined if you only have one purpose. Although you will try your best, it will not be entirely within your control to achieve the purpose of your project. In the example given here, you might be unable to influence the department or practice to institute new stress management systems, even though you and others have undertaken the preliminary work that demonstrates the need.
- *Step 3*. Define the *outcomes* for achieving the purpose of the 'project'. These are what you want the project to achieve – the specific end results that will be achieved when the planned activities are carried out. An example might be *to be competent in assertiveness skills*. Achieving the outcomes should be within your control.

- *Step 4.* Define the *activities* that you will undertake in order to achieve each outcome, and the resources available. Activities define how you will carry out your project. Examples might be *keep stress log* or *attend assertiveness training course*. You should expect to undertake three to seven activities for every outcome you hope to accomplish (*see* Table 6.2 for an example).

The log-frame structure is based on the concept of cause and effect. The vertical logic is based on a sequence of causal relationships starting from the bottom upwards. There is a logical relationship between activities and outcomes, outcomes and the purpose, and the purpose and the goal. Therefore *if* specific activities are carried out *then* certain outcomes will be produced. If the outcomes you describe are produced, then the declared purpose will be achieved. If the purpose is achieved, your goal should be attained. So from the bottom upwards:

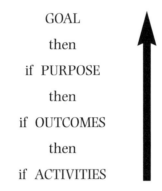

GOAL

then

if PURPOSE

then

if OUTCOMES

then

if ACTIVITIES

Evaluate your results sequentially, from the bottom upwards. You cannot logically evaluate the *outcomes* of your activities without first monitoring whether the *activities* have been carried out and achieved as planned. Similarly, you cannot expect to obtain the improvements described in your *purpose* without the *outcomes* having been achieved first.

The horizontal logic

Horizontal logic underlies the way in which you measure the effectiveness of your plan. Specify how you will measure progress for each of the four levels of the vertical logic – the activities, outcomes, purpose and goal. As far as possible, use concrete terms rather than vague measures as tangible indicators of progress. These indicators should have the following qualities.

- They clearly describe how the achievement of the activity, outcome or purpose contributes to the success of the project.

- They focus on what is important for the purpose or overall goal.
- They clearly relate to the activity, outcome, purpose or goal with which they are associated.
- They are of sufficient number and detailed enough to measure activities, outcomes, purpose and goal adequately.
- They are specific to an activity, outcome, purpose or goal.
- They are objectively verifiable, so that two independent observers measure achievement in the same way – quantitative or qualitative in nature.

The indicator might be direct (e.g. numbers of days of sickness absence) or indirect (e.g. number of staff attending a stress management training course).
    These indicators, like others elsewhere, should be *SMART*:

- **S**pecific
- **M**easurable
- **A**chievable
- **R**ealistic
- **T**ime-limited.

Then decide how you will verify that all of the specified indicators have been achieved. You might gather simple data as part of your project, or refer to sources of information such as reports, surveys, official documents, notes of meetings or a review of case studies over time.

Box 6.1

For each level of the vertical logic there will be a set of objectively verifiable indicators which are appropriate to the objectives at that level and which constitute proof of achievement at that level.[94]

Important assumptions

You know that it is very unlikely that your plans will go forward without a hitch, but that doesn't stop you assuming that you will progress smoothly. In reality, things that you have not expected crop up to obstruct or delay your progress.
    The assumptions that you describe in your log frame include factors or conditions that could affect your progress with the project or its overall success, over which you have no or only limited control. For the overseas development projects with which the log frame has been used, these might include external factors such as unexpected bad weather or an earthquake.

For you, thinking of implementing a stress management programme, examples of major external factors that are beyond your control include new Government imperatives about further health service reorganisations or the passing of new health and safety legislation. More minor assumptions might be the extent of co-operation that is forthcoming from other members of your team or the managers in your department or practice or trust. These will affect whether you are able to undertake many of the activities you plan, or to achieve the outcomes or purpose in your log frame.

As well as the unexpected factors that might spoil your plans, you may be assuming too much. For example, it may be that you and others in your team have insufficient knowledge and skills to carry out the activities that you envisage, or you might not have forecast the extent of resources needed to implement your ideas.

There may be other risks to your planned timetable, too. You may not have thought through the consequences of your plans – the opportunity costs if you switch the way in which resources are allocated (time, effort, money, etc.) to be in line with your plans. Alternatively, you may not have predicted the new stress-provoking factors which might arise from the revised systems and procedures that you establish in the course of carrying out your plan.

Getting started

Read through the series of steps below and work through the thinking behind the way in which we have put the log frame together. Before you start, note down all of the people who will have some influence on the progress or viability of your stress management plan throughout the lifetime of your 'project'. They might include the following:

- other team members
- your partner and family at home
- friends with whom you socialise or play sport
- managers in your department, practice or trust
- staff at work to whom you delegate work
- people who delegate work to you
- people for whom you are responsible
- your cleaner or gardener at home
- relatives who are dependent on you, etc.

You will need to anticipate how they will influence your plan – to enhance or limit progress. So consider how they will interact with you and include them in the activities of your log frame, or in the assumptions that you make. You will be taking account of their influence – by harnessing their help or preventing them from obstructing you – in the nature of the activities that you include in your plan.

The worked example that we shall develop below illustrates the processes that you need to adopt to make up a log frame. The contents of the example log frame are an illustration of the thinking behind a log frame, and are not prescriptive. You should use the evolving framework as a guide, rather than lifting the example 'off the peg' for your own requirements. Much of the learning and benefits from a log frame arise from the preparatory work involved in putting it together and thinking through the factors that are individual to you, that will enhance or prevent your progress. They will be unique to you, your networks of individuals and your circumstances.

We have not included every detail of the possible assumptions or potential risks that might occur during such a project plan, or even the numerous activities that you could undertake. To do so would have resulted in such a vast amount of background detail that it would be difficult for the reader to distinguish 'must do' information from 'could do' detail. You will be able to include more minor information about risks and assumptions yourself. The columns of a completed log frame that is undertaken over a period of a year or more often stretch to over three or four sides of A4 paper.[97]

Have a first go at establishing the vertical logic.

- *Step 1*. Have a go at writing down the goal of your 'project'. In Table 6.1, this is *to minimise stress in my working life*. You might want to take a wider view and consider that your ultimate goal is to provide better healthcare for patients and the community, or to be a much happier person at work and at home.
- *Step 2*. Have a go at writing down the purpose of your 'project'. In Table 6.1, this is *to implement new stress management systems and programme.*
- *Step 3*. Have a go at writing down the outcomes of your 'project' that taken together will achieve your purpose. These are really intermediate achievements in your progress plan. In Table 6.1, these are *competent in assertiveness skills, protected time for activities outside work, stress management plan for department/practice agreed*, and *reorganisation of team's working practices agreed.* Now you need to challenge yourself. Are there gaps? Are these four outcomes appropriate for your purpose?
- *Step 4*. Have a go at writing down the activities that you initially think might achieve each outcome. In Table 6.1, these include *attend assertiveness training, keep a log of your workload, review stressors at work* and *hold department/practice meeting.*

Now you should apply the 'if-then' logic described previously to test out the cause and effect relationship. *If* these activities are carried out, *then* you will achieve these outcomes. *If* you attend a training course on assertiveness, *then* you will be competent in assertiveness. You can see that the case is crumbling – there are missing links.

You will have to do more than simply attend an assertiveness training course. You will have to practise being assertive to become competent and improve with feedback from others about your assertiveness technique. You have been assuming that attending a training course is all that you need to do, whereas in fact in addition to activities such as practising the skills you have learned, you should have undertaken linked activities, such as prioritising learning about assertiveness skills, locating an appropriate training course, setting aside time to go, justifying the course fees, etc.

Table 6.1: Step 1 of building up the log frame to reduce stress at work for you: your first attempt at planning your vertical logical pathway

	Summary	Indicators	Verification	Assumptions
Goal	To minimise stress in my working life			
Purpose	To implement new stress management systems and programme			
Outcomes (intermediate achievements)	Competent in assertiveness skills Protected time for activities outside work Stress management plan for department/practice agreed Reorganisation of team's working practices agreed			
Activities	Attend assertiveness training Keep a log of your workload Review stressors at work Hold department/practice meeting			

Look again at these activities and outcomes. *If* you review your stressors at work and undertake a job satisfaction audit, *then* ... what? The outcomes described in Table 6.1 were about finding protected time for activities outside work and agreeing a stress management plan as a department or practice team. There are *no* intermediate steps in the list of activities for converting the information gathered in the review of stress or job satisfaction audit to controlling the stressors identified or boosting job satisfaction, and *no* specific outcomes, so you need to add some more activities, as we do **in bold** in Table 6.2.

Numbering the outcomes and the activities linked to them will help you to see how *if* you undertake certain activities *then* you will achieve specific outcomes, as in Table 6.2. Making these linkages has highlighted the fact that further activities have to be undertaken in order to achieve the outcomes, as indicated by the suggestions added **in bold** in Table 6.2.

Table 6.2: Step 2 of building up the log frame to reduce stress at work for you: linking activities with outputs

	Summary	Indicators	Verification	Assumptions
Goal	To minimise stress in my working life			
Purpose	To implement new stress management systems and programme			
Outcomes (intermediate achievements)	1 Competent in assertiveness skills 2 Protected time for activities outside work 3 Stress management plan for department/practice agreed 4 Reorganisation of team's working practices agreed			
Activities	**1.1 Compose a personal development plan and prioritise assertiveness** **1.2 Arrange to learn about assertiveness; find resources to provide cover and course fee, locate training course** 1.3 Attend assertiveness training course **1.4 Practise assertiveness with team and patients; obtain feedback from team** **2.1 Keep a log of workload and activities outside work** **2.2 Discuss time/activities log with colleagues at work and family at home; make a plan for non-work activities** **2.3 Join a health club and attend induction** **2.4 Review diary and write in non-work activities** 3.1 Keep a stress log both at work and outside work (*see* page 28) **3.2 Review stressors at work as individual and as team** 3.3 Review stressors at home as individual and with partner/family **3.4 Conduct audit of own job satisfaction** **3.5 Discuss stressors and job satisfaction with colleagues at work and partner at home**			

Table 6.2: Continued				
	Summary	*Indicators*	*Verification*	*Assumptions*
	3.6 Arrange meeting with work colleagues to compose stress management plan for team as a whole			
	4.1 Manager reviews hours worked by team members, their roles and responsibilities, and their skill mix vs. their competencies			
	4.2 Keep own record of work done and potential for delegation or discontinuity of work			
	4.3 Call team meeting, including manager and staff, to discuss changes to working practices			

Now that you are beginning to get the vertical logic in place, you should start thinking out what assumptions you have been making, and if there are any potential risks associated with your logical plan. Once you have recognised these, you may have to add in other activities in order to minimise the effects of previously unforeseen external factors. This is the stage when you should be anticipating problems that could interrupt the progress of your project action plan. You may have a blind spot about these possible problem areas, so you could usefully discuss the preliminary thinking of your project plan with someone else who might point out weaknesses you have not yet recognised, or give you information about possible external influences of which you were unaware.

The additions **in bold** in Table 6.3 provide some examples of assumptions that you might be making. You can see that as you think through how you are going to undertake these activities and turn them into outcomes, some gaps are appearing – you may be assuming that you already possess the knowledge and skills necessary to compose a personal development plan, or that you or your manager are capable of undertaking a review of your stressors at work.

The types of risks that may arise include the following: you waste your time attending an assertiveness skills course that does not fit your needs; you identify topics that you urgently need to learn more about, and you therefore cannot justify learning more about assertiveness; you cannot find the right course

Table 6.3: Step 3 of building up the log frame to reduce stress at work for you: adding in assumptions about your planned activities

	Summary	Indicators	Verification	Assumptions
Goal	To minimise stress in your working life			
Purpose	To implement new stress management systems and programme			
Outcomes (intermediate achievements)	1 Competent in assertiveness skills 2 Protected time for activities outside work 3 Stress management plan for department/ practice agreed 4 Reorganisation of team's working practices agreed			
Activities	1.1 Compose a personal development plan (PDP) and prioritise assertiveness 1.2 Arrange to learn about assertiveness; find resources to provide cover and course fee; locate training course 1.3 Attend assertiveness training course 1.4 Practise assertiveness with team and patients; obtain feedback from team 2.1 Keep a log of workload and activities outside work 2.2 Discuss time/activities log with colleagues at work and family at home. Make a plan for non-work activities 2.3 Join a health club			**1.1 You know how to compose a PDP/identify learning needs** **1.2 Resources will be forthcoming; course will be accessible and available** **1.3 Assertiveness can be learned by attending a training course** **1.4 Practising on team prepares you for the real world; you can become competent within the timescale of the project plan** **2.1 You have the time and skills to organise a workload and time/ activities survey** **2.2 Colleagues and family will be interested and willing to help** **2.3 A health club is local to you; the health club ambience appeals to you**

Table 6.3:   Continued

Summary	Indicators	Verification	Assumptions
2.4 Review diary and write in non-work activities			**2.4 Commitments that have already been made allow inclusion of non-work activities; you are assertive enough with yourself to prioritise non-work activities**
3.1 Keep a stress log both at work and outside work (*see* page 28)			**3.1 You have the skills to keep a stress log**
3.2 Review stressors at work as individual and as team			**3.2 Colleagues at work are interested and willing to become engaged**
3.3 Review stressors at home as individual and with partner/family			**3.3 Family and partner at home are willing to be engaged**
3.4 Conduct audit of own job satisfaction			**3.4 You know of a validated scale of job satisfaction**
3.5 Discuss stressors and job satisfaction with colleagues at work and partner at home			**3.5 Colleagues at work and family are willing to be engaged in this discussion**
3.6 Arrange meeting with work colleagues to compose stress management plan for team as a whole			**3.6 Colleagues at work are willing to make and own plan and find solutions**
4.1 Manager reviews hours worked by team members, their roles/responsibilities, and their skill mix vs. their competencies			**4.1 Manager has the skills and time to review working practices of team members**
4.2 Keep own record of workload and potential for delegation or discontinuity of work			**4.2 You have the skills and time to review workload and detect potential for delegation**
4.3 Team meeting, including staff and manager, to discuss changes to working practices			**4.3 Team is willing to co-operate with regard to changing working practices**

that is pitched at an appropriate level for you, held at a convenient time and afford-able. Other areas of risk will include the following: staff numbers remain stable; no significant new Government directives, etc., are issued that overturn your priorities at work; no crisis occurs at your workplace (e.g. a flood or fire).

So the next step is to add yet more activities to anticipate the risks that you now realise could happen, and to reduce the likelihood of them occurring and obstructing your progress with your plan. The risks and activities shown **in bold** in Table 6.4 illustrate a variety of risks that might occur and activities that you might adopt in order to minimise the effects of these risks on your progress and minimise the stresses in your life.

The next step is to move on to specify the assumptions that you are making about achieving your outcomes. Examples of these have been added **in bold** in Table 6.5.

For instance, you may assume that you can identify all of the significant stressors that are impinging on you by keeping a stress log, whereas in fact you need a parallel review by someone else to give a different perspective and more objective information on the extent of stress arising from aspects of the organisation or the various team members, of which you were previously unaware. So consider adding another 'activity', such as a review of work-related stress by an external consultant or peer. There will also be a potential risk that in minimising or controlling the identified sources of stress, you create new stresses that are at least as bad as the original stressor – perhaps you control a stress for you by delegating work to one of the others in the team, but as they do not have the time or training for the additional work, more chaos is created. The team 'awayday' which you have already added as an activity might be an opportunity to discuss ways in which the team as a whole, rather than you alone, can control stress at work for team members as a whole.

Now it is time to map out the assumptions and risks associated with your purpose and overall goal. We have started this process in the additions shown **in bold** in Table 6.6, but in reality you would have far more to add to these sections. You need to think of any external factors that are required, or that might prevent the long-term sustainability of your goal or purpose, for the project to be successful.

You will also need to think about the 'potential risks' that are likely to arise. The assumptions that you are making and the risks you anticipate should trigger you to add extra activities and outcomes to your right-hand column in real life. We have *not* added any extra activities or outcomes here in our example log frame in Table 6.6 for the sake of simplicity, but you will certainly have to do so in order to take adequate measures to ensure your smooth progress with your plan.

Your final step will be to describe the indicators for all of your activities, outcomes, purpose and goal, as well as the means by which you can verify

continued on page 129

Table 6.4: Step 4 of building up the log frame to reduce stress at work for you: add more activities to anticipate the 'risks' that may arise from previously planned activities and assumptions

	Summary	Indicators	Verification	Assumptions *and* **Risks**
Goal	To minimise stress in your working life			
Purpose	To implement new stress management systems and programme			
Outcomes (intermediate achievements)	1 Competent in assertiveness skills 2 Protected time for activities outside work 3 Stress management plan for department/practice agreed 4 Reorganisation of team's working practices agreed			
Activities	1.1 Compose a personal development plan (PDP) and prioritise assertiveness 1.2 Arrange to learn about assertiveness; find resources to provide cover and course fee; locate training course 1.3 Attend assertiveness training course 1.4 Practise assertiveness with team and patients; obtain feedback from team **1.5 Obtain course curriculum and talk to someone who has been to the proposed assertiveness training course to find out more about it** 2.1 Keep a log of workload and activities outside work			*Assumptions* 1.1 You know how to compose a PDP/identify learning needs 1.2 Resources will be forthcoming; course will be accessible and available 1.3 Assertiveness can be learned by attending a training course 1.4 Practising on team prepares you for the real world; you can become competent within the timescale of the project plan *Risks* **1.5 Assertiveness course is inappropriate for you** *Assumptions* 2.1 You have the time and skills to organise a workload and time/activities survey

Table 6.4: Continued

Summary	Indicators	Verification	Assumptions *and* **Risks**
2.2 Discuss time/activities log with colleagues at work and family at home. Make a plan for non-work activities			2.2 Colleagues and family will be interested and willing to help
2.3 Join a health club			2.3 A health club is local to you; the health club ambience appeals to you
2.4 Review diary and write in non-work activities			2.4 Commitments that have already been made allow inclusion of non-work activities; you are assertive enough with yourself to prioritise non-work activities
			Risks
2.5 Visit several health clubs and try sample days before joining one as a member			**2.5 You do not like the ethos of the health club and rarely go to it**
2.6 Agree with siblings how to help parent who is ill			**2.6 One of your parents becomes ill and you have to spend non-work time helping them**
			Assumptions
3.1 Keep a stress log both at work and outside work (*see* page 28)			3.1 You have the skills to keep a stress log
3.2 Review stressors at work as individual and as team			3.2 Colleagues at work are interested and willing to become engaged
3.3 Review stressors at home as individual and with partner/family			3.3 Family and partner at home are willing to be engaged
3.4 Conduct audit of own job satisfaction			3.4 You know of a validated scale of job satisfaction
3.5 Discuss stressors and job satisfaction with colleagues at work and partner at home			3.5 Colleagues at work and family are willing to be engaged in this discussion
3.6 Arrange meeting with work colleagues to compose stress management plan for team as a whole			3.6 Colleagues at work are willing to make and own plan and find solutions

Table 6.4: Continued

Summary	Indicators	Verification	Assumptions *and Risks*
3.7 Arrangements for meetings with colleagues to discuss stress management optimise their attendance (e.g. with lunch, at breakfast meeting, when other priorities are being discussed)			*Risks* **3.7 Colleagues cancel meetings you arrange to discuss stress management**
4.1 Manager reviews hours worked by team members, their roles/responsibilities, and their skill mix vs. their competencies			*Assumptions* 4.1 Manager has the skills and time to review working practices of team members
4.2 Keep own record of workload and potential for delegation or discontinuity of work			4.2 You have the skills and time to review workload and detect potential for delegation
4.3 Team meeting, including staff and manager, to discuss changes to working practices			4.3 Team is willing to co-operate with regard to changing working practices
4.4 You and manager implement plan to retain staff (boosting staff morale and job satisfaction, with incentives)			*Risks* **4.4 Staff leave, and staff turnover is high**
4.5 You and colleagues insist on team 'awayday' with manager to discuss results of review and draw up a consensus plan for changing working practices			**4.5 Manager has biased perspective about the review**

Table 6.5: Step 5 of building up the log frame to reduce stress at work for you: adding assumptions that you are making about expected outcomes and adding more activities to reduce the likelihood of potential risk occurring

	Summary	Indicators	Verification	Assumptions and Risks
Goal	To minimise stress in your working life			
Purpose	To implement new stress management systems and programme			
Outcomes (intermediate achievements)	1 Competent in assertiveness skills			*Assumptions* **1.1 You apply your new knowledge and skills in assertiveness consistently, whatever the provocation**
	2 Protected time for activities outside work			**2.1 Your weekly schedule is typical and does not have unforeseen 'crises' that disrupt it** **2.2 You have activities outside work that you enjoy**
	3 Stress management plan for department/ practice agreed			**3.1 You can control the sources of stress that you identify as a team** **3.2 Your own individual stresses can be minimised as one part of a team plan** **3.3 You have identified all major sources of stress that impinge on team members and on yourself** *Risks* **3.4 You create new stresses that are at least as bad as the original stressor as a result of changes to working practices**

Table 6.5: Continued

	Summary	Indicators	Verification	Assumptions and Risks
	4　Reorganisation of team's working practices agreed			*Assumptions* **4.1 Consensus is possible and staff agree to their job descriptions being revised** **4.2 Revised working practices are possible even when current staff leave** **4.3 Agreed new working practices are possible even if there are staff vacancies**
Activities	1.1 Compose a personal development plan (PDP) and prioritise assertiveness 1.2 Arrange to learn about assertiveness; find resources to provide cover and course fee; locate training course 1.3 Attend assertiveness training course 1.4 Practise assertiveness with team and patients; obtain feedback from team 1.5 Obtain course curriculum and talk to someone who has been to the proposed assertiveness training course to find out more about it **1.6 Monitor extent of assertiveness at a later date** 2.1 Keep a log of workload and activities outside work 2.2 Discuss time/activities log with colleagues at work and family at home. Make a plan for non-work activities			*Assumptions* 1.1 You know how to compose a PDP/ identify learning needs 1.2 Resources will be forthcoming; course will be accessible and available 1.3 Assertiveness can be learned by attending a training course 1.4 Practising on team prepares you for the real world; you can become competent within the timescale of the project plan *Risks* 1.5 Assertiveness course is inappropriate for you *Assumptions* 2.1 You have the time and skills to organise a workload and time/activities survey 2.2 Colleagues and family will be interested and willing to help

Table 6.5: Continued

Summary	Indicators	Verification	Assumptions and Risks
2.3 Join a health club			2.3 A health club is local to you; the health club ambience appeals to you
2.4 Review diary and write in non-work activities			2.4 Commitments that have already been made allow inclusion of non-work activities; you are assertive enough with yourself to prioritise non-work activities
			Risks
2.5 Visit several health clubs			2.5 You do not like the ethos of the health club and rarely go to it
2.6 Agree with siblings how to help parent who is ill			2.6 One of your parents becomes ill and you have to spend non-work time helping them
2.7 Take up new hobby you have always intended to pursue			
3.1 Keep a stress log both at work and outside work (*see* page 28)			*Assumptions* 3.1 You have the skills to keep a stress log
3.2 Review stressors at work as individual and as team			3.2 Colleagues at work are interested and willing to become engaged
3.3 Review stressors at home as individual and with partner/family			3.3 Family and partner at home are willing to be engaged
3.4 Conduct audit of own job satisfaction			3.4 You know of a validated scale of job satisfaction
3.5 Discuss stressors and job satisfaction with colleagues at work and partner at home			3.5 Colleagues at work and family are willing to be engaged in this discussion
3.6 Arrange meeting with work colleagues to compose stress management plan for team as a whole			3.6 Colleagues at work are willing to make and own plan and find solutions
3.7 Arrangements for meetings with colleagues to discuss stress management optimise their attendance (e.g. with lunch, at breakfast meeting, when other priorities are being discussed)			*Risks* 3.7 Colleagues cancel meetings you arrange to discuss stress management

Table 6.5: Continued

Summary	Indicators	Verification	Assumptions and Risks
3.8 Commission an external review of stressors in your department/practice in relation to teamworking and working practices			
3.9 Undertake a repeat audit of stressors for you and the team as a follow-up to changed working practices			
			Assumptions
4.1 Manager reviews hours worked by team members, their roles/responsibilities, and their skill mix vs. their competencies			4.1 Manager has the skills and time to review working practices of team members
4.2 Keep own record of workload and potential for delegation or discontinuity of work			4.2 You have the skills and time to review workload and detect potential for delegation
4.3 Team meeting, including staff and manager to discuss changes to working practices			4.3 Team is willing to co-operate with regard to changing working practices
			Risks
4.4 You and manager implement plan to retain staff (boosting staff morale and job satisfaction, with incentives)			4.4 Staff leave, and staff turnover is high
4.5 You and colleagues insist on team 'awayday' with manager to discuss results of review and draw up a consensus plan for changing working practices. **You agree stress management plan at awayday, taking into account the results of the internal and external stress reviews**			4.5 Manager has biased perspective about the review

Table 6.6: Step 6 of building up the log frame to reduce stress at work for you: adding various assumptions that you are making about your purpose and goal

	Summary	Indicators	Verification	Assumptions and Risks
Goal	1 To minimise stress in your working life			*Assumptions* 1.1 You remain working (in your current post) 1.2 You are able to thrive both as a person and as a health professional 1.3 You are, and remain, in good health *Risks* 1.4 Other significant life events occur 1.5 Your job does not exist in the future as a result of NHS changes
Purpose	1 To implement new stress management systems and programme			*Assumptions* 1.1 You remain working (in your current post) 1.2 You have the resources to implement the stress management systems and programme 1.3 The expected stress management systems and programme are effective in reducing stress for you and the team *Risks* 1.4 The NHS or your overarching organisation require new systems or work that create new stresses and conflict with your revised systems and ways of working 1.5 Your practice/department is forced to combine with another that has a different culture

Table 6.6: Continued

	Summary	Indicators	Verification	Assumptions and Risks
Outcomes (intermediate achievements)	1 Competent in assertiveness skills			*Assumptions* 1.1 You apply your new knowledge and skills in assertiveness consistently, whatever the provocation
	2 Protected time for activities outside work			2.1 Your weekly schedule is typical and does not have unforeseen 'crises' that disrupt it 2.2 You have activities outside work that you enjoy
	3 Stress management plan for department/ practice agreed			3.1 You can control the sources of stress that you identify as a team 3.2 Your own individual stresses can be minimised as one part of a team plan 3.3 You have identified all major sources of stress that impinge on team members and on yourself *Risks* 3.4 You create new stresses that are at least as bad as the original stressor as a result of changes to working practices
	4 Reorganisation of team's working practices agreed **You add other outcomes to address the assumptions and risks with regard to purpose and goal**			*Assumptions* 4.1 Consensus is possible and staff agree to their job descriptions being revised 4.2 Revised working practices are possible even when current staff leave 4.3 Agreed new working practices are possible even if there are staff vacancies

Table 6.6: Continued

Summary	Indicators	Verification	Assumptions and Risks
Activities			
1.1 Compose a personal development plan (PDP) and prioritise assertiveness			*Assumptions* 1.1 You know how to compose a PDP/ identify learning needs
1.2 Arrange to learn about assertiveness; find resources to provide cover and course fee; locate training course			1.2 Resources will be forthcoming; course will be accessible and available
1.3 Attend assertiveness training course			1.3 Assertiveness can be learned by attending a training course
1.4 Practise assertiveness with team and patients; obtain feedback from team			1.4 Practising on team prepares you for the real world; you can become competent within the timescale of the project plan
1.5 Obtain course curriculum and talk to someone who has been to the proposed assertiveness training course to find out more about it			*Risks* 1.5 Assertiveness course is inappropriate for you
1.6 Monitor extent of assertiveness at a later date			
2.1 Keep a log of workload and activities outside work			*Assumptions* 2.1 You have the time and skills to organise a workload and time/activities survey
2.2 Discuss time/activities log with colleagues at work and family at home. Make a plan for non-work activities			2.2 Colleagues and family will be interested and willing to help
2.3 Join a health club			2.3 Local health club has an ambience that appeals to you
2.4 Review diary and write in non-work activities			2.4 Commitments that have already been made allow inclusion of non-work activities; you are assertive enough with yourself to prioritise non-work activities

Table 6.6: Continued

Summary	Indicators	Verification	Assumptions and Risks
2.5 Visit several health clubs			*Risks*
			2.5 You do not like the ethos of the health club and rarely go to it
2.6 Agree with siblings how to help parent who is ill			2.6 One of your parents becomes ill and you have to spend non-work time helping them
2.7 Take up new hobby you have always intended to pursue			
3.1 Keep a stress log both at work and outside work (*see* page 28)			*Assumptions*
			3.1 You have the skills to keep a stress log
3.2 Review stressors at work as individual and as team			3.2 Colleagues at work are interested and willing to become engaged
3.3 Review stressors at home as individual and with partner/family			3.3 Family and partner at home are willing to be engaged
3.4 Conduct audit of own job satisfaction			3.4 You know of a validated scale of job satisfaction
3.5 Discuss stressors and job satisfaction with colleagues at work and partner at home			3.5 Colleagues at work and family are willing to be engaged in this discussion
3.6 Arrange meeting with work colleagues to compose stress management plan for team as a whole			3.6 Colleagues at work are willing to make and own plan and find solutions
3.7 Arrangements for meetings with colleagues to discuss stress management. Optimise their attendance (e.g. with lunch, at breakfast meeting, when other priorities are being discussed)			*Risks* 3.7 Colleagues cancel meetings you arrange to discuss stress management
3.8 Commission an external review of stressors in your department/practice in relation to teamworking and working practices			

Table 6.6: Continued

Summary	Indicators	Verification	Assumptions and Risks
3.9 Undertake a repeat audit of stressors for you and the team as a follow-up to changed working practices			
4.1 Manager reviews hours worked by team members, their roles/responsibilities, and their skill mix vs. their competencies			*Assumptions* 4.1 Manager has the skills and time to review working practices of team members
4.2 Keep own record of workload and potential for delegation or discontinuity of work			4.2 You have the skills and time to review workload and detect potential for delegation
4.3 Team meeting, including staff and manager, to discuss changes to working practices			4.3 Team is willing to co-operate with regard to changing working practices
4.4 You and manager implement plan to retain staff (boosting staff morale and job satisfaction, with incentives)			*Risks* 4.4 Staff leave, and staff turnover is high
4.5 You and colleagues insist on team 'awayday' with manager to discuss results of review and draw up a consensus plan for changing working practices. You agree stress management plan at awayday, taking into account the results of the internal and external stress reviews			4.5 Manager has biased perspective about the review
You add other activities to address the assumptions and risks with regard to purpose and goal			

that you have achieved them. You should also add a timescale for each indicator. The indicators should be achievable and worthwhile. Turn back to page 108 to remind yourself of the ideal characteristics of indicators.

The examples added to Table 6.7 are shown **in bold.** They illustrate how someone might do their best to fix appropriate indicators and give examples of how the indicators might be verified.

Concluding your logical plan

Now that you have finished mapping out your log frame, you should refine it and perhaps discuss it with someone else to see whether it is realistic, or whether there is something else that you have not thought of.

Decide how often you are going to review the log frame. A six-monthly review, say, should enable you to keep track of your progress with your project. The extent to which you meet the indicators should give you a good idea of how you are getting on. You may then also realise that there are additional assumptions and risks that you have not previously thought of or addressed.

Table 6.7: Step 7 of building up the log frame to reduce stress at work for you: adding indicators and the means of verification of progress for your planned activities, outcomes, purpose and goal

	Summary	Indicators (examples)	Verification (examples)	Assumptions and Risks
Goal	1 To minimise stress in your working life	1 Feeling of well-being for majority of time at work	1 Follow-up review of your stress log shows reduced frequency and extent of stressors arising from work	As for Table 6.6
Purpose	1 To implement new stress management systems and programme	1.1 Co-ordinated stress management in place across workplace by all staff by 6 months 1.2 Agreed milestones representing reduced stress levels in (i) team (ii) you	1.1 Few errors or adverse events recorded in monitoring of systems 1.2 Follow-up review with (i) work colleagues and (ii) your partner at home shows that milestones are reached and your expected coping methods are in place	As for Table 6.6
Outcomes (intermediate achievements)	1 Competent in assertiveness skills 2 Protected time for activities outside work	1.1 Act assertively with patients and colleagues consistently after you have been on course 2.1 Regular sport activities and hobbies included in weekly schedule 2.2 Learned to play musical instrument by one year	1.1 Feedback about the extent of your assertiveness given at annual peer appraisal 2.1 Your diary shows how you spent time on sport and hobbies included at least three times a week, every week, in the first six months 2.2 Good enough to play musical instrument with friends	As for Table 6.6

Table 6.7: Continued

	Summary	Indicators (examples)	Verification (examples)	Assumptions and Risks
3	Stress management plan for department/practice agreed	3.1 Team at work agreed stress management plan by (date) 3.2 Changes made at work in line with stress management plan 3.3 Staff incentive scheme boosts job satisfaction by x months	3.1 Stress management steering group set up and put timed plan into action 3.2 Staff forum set up to discuss and debrief on stress issues 3.3 Reduced staff turnover; repeat staff survey shows improved job satisfaction	
4	Reorganisation of team's working practices agreed	4.1 New skill mix for delivery of certain services by x months 4.2 Team members have revised roles 4.3 New working practices in place by x months	4.1 Audits of care pathways demonstrate that team delivers services as agreed 4.2 Team members' job descriptions revised to reflect new roles 4.3 New systems and procedures in place, with audit programme	
	Other outcomes to address the assumptions and risks with regard to purpose and goal			
Activities	1.1 Compose a personal development plan (PDP) and prioritise assertiveness 1.2 Arrange to learn about assertiveness; find resources to provide cover and course fee; locate training course 1.3 Obtain course curriculum and talk to someone who has been to the proposed assertiveness training course to find out more about it 1.4 Attend assertiveness training course	1.1 PDP drawn up; learning needs prioritised 1.2 Course booked by x months; bid to training budget for course fee 1.3 Find 'right' person who has been to course 1.4 Assertiveness course attended by x months	1.1 PDP approved at annual appraisal 1.2 Application made; bid for course fee successful 1.3 Decided to go to course after good insight from ex-course member 1.4 Certificate of course attendance obtained	As for Table 6.6

Table 6.7: Continued

Summary	Indicators (examples)	Verification (examples)	Assumptions and Risks
1.5 Practise assertiveness with team and patients; obtain feedback from team	1.5 Feedback forms completed by team by x months	1.5 Discussion of feedback with trusted colleague	
1.6 Monitor extent of assertiveness at a later date	1.6 Assertiveness demonstrated in significant event audit by x months	1.6 Significant event audit demonstrating assertiveness included in PDP	
2.1 Keep a log of workload and activities outside work	2.1 Log completed by x months demonstrates how time was spent at work and outside work	2.1 Workload log included as underpinning evidence in PDP	
2.2 Discuss time/activities log with colleagues at work and family at home. Make a plan for non-work activities	2.2 Plan emerged within three months of discussions	2.2 Several colleagues and also your partner at home discuss your log with you; discussion cited in PDP	
2.3 Join a health club	2.3 Attend induction at health club one week after joining	2.3 Membership fee paid; baseline record of fitness completed	
2.4 Review diary and write in non-work activities	2.4 Spaces made in weekly timetable from one month onwards	2.4 Entries for non-work activities written in diary six months ahead	
2.5 Visit several health clubs	2.5 Try sample days at two health clubs before joining one as member	2.5 Day spent at two health clubs	
2.6 Agree with siblings how to help parent who is ill	2.6 Agreed rota with siblings for helping parent who is ill	2.6 Entries made on your home calendar for your turn with helping your parent; employ domestic or carer help	
2.7 Take up new hobby you have always intended to pursue	2.7 Learn a musical instrument; practise for lessons by x months	2.7 Buy a musical instrument; attend music lessons	

Table 6.7:   Continued

Summary	Indicators (examples)	Verification (examples)	Assumptions and Risks
3.1 Keep a stress log both at work and outside work (*see* page 28)	**3.1 Completed stress log by *x* months**	**3.1 Summary of stress log included in PDP**	
3.2 Review stressors at work as individual and as team	**3.2 Reducing stress is topic of staff meeting by *x* months**	**3.2 Staff meeting convened to discuss review of stress log**	
3.3 Review stressors at home as individual and with partner/family	**3.3 Reducing stress is topic of family meeting by *x* months**	**3.3 Reducing stress is topic of convened meeting with all family at home**	
3.4 Conduct audit of own job satisfaction	**3.4 Completed audit of own job satisfaction by *x* months**	**3.4 Method of rating job satisfaction shared with others at work**	
3.5 Discuss stressors and job satisfaction with colleagues at work and partner at home	**3.5 Include in 3.2 above summary of positive factors to boost job satisfaction**	**3.5 Boosting job satisfaction and potential change of work discussed with partner at home**	
3.6 Arrange meeting with work colleagues to compose stress management plan for team as a whole	**3.6 Include in 3.2 above or at follow-up meeting by *x* months**	**3.6 Include in 3.2 above or at follow-up meeting**	
3.7 Arrangements for meetings with colleagues to discuss stress management optimise their attendance (e.g. with lunch, at breakfast meeting, when other priorities are being discussed)	**3.7 Hold meeting by x months**	**3.7 At least 75% of colleagues attend meeting**	
3.8 Commission an external review of stressors in your department/practice in relation to teamworking and working practices	**3.8 External review conducted by *x* months**	**3.8 Comprehensive report from external reviewer of stresses with regard to teamworking and working practices**	
3.9 Undertake a repeat audit of stressors for you and the team as a follow-up to changed working practices	**3.9 Repeat audit by x months**	**3.9 Repeat audit results of stressors, reviewed as a team and further action planned in notes of meeting**	

Table 6.7: Continued

Summary	Indicators (examples)	Verification (examples)	Assumptions and Risks
4.1 Manager reviews hours worked by team members, their roles/responsibilities, and their skill mix vs. their competencies	**4.1 Review undertaken by *x* months**	**4.1 Manager publishes review and invites input from staff**	
4.2 Keep own record of workload and potential for delegation or discontinuity of work	**4.2 Colleagues review and discuss your log of workload and associated plan**	**4.2 Notes of colleagues' critique of your log and plan to delegate/ discontinue work from team meeting**	
4.3 Team meeting, including staff and manager, to discuss changes to working practices	**4.3 Plan for changed working practices made by *x* months**	**4.3 Revised work diary sheets for team members; revised organisational systems in place**	
4.4 You and manager implement plan to retain staff (boosting staff morale and job satisfaction, with incentives)	**4.4 Retention plan for department/ practice agreed by *x* months**	**4.4 Retention plan for department/practice published in business plan**	
4.5 Run team 'awayday' to discuss results of working practices review, a consensus plan for changing working practices, and stress management	**4.5 Team's awayday held; democratic plan agreed**	**4.5 Notes of action points from team's awayday; majority of team attended awayday**	
Other activities to address the assumptions and risks with regard to purpose and goal			

Reflecting on what you have read and learned about

You have come a long way since you first opened this book and started to read it through from the beginning.

You will have begun to recognise and understand the physical and psychological symptoms of stress in you, which is an important first step in coping with them. If you do not understand how the symptoms of stress are manifested in you, you may misinterpret them as signs of a serious illness, such as a brain tumour or other life-threatening disease. You will remember that stress symptoms in the short term *cannot harm you*. The effects of stress over the long term cause a gradual deterioration of your general health that *can be corrected*.

There are a range of things that you can do to help yourself, which we described comprehensively in Chapter 3. You might experiment with the methods we discussed there, so that you find different ways of minimising stress at work or coping with its effects on you.

However, you are not alone – you are one of a team working in the health service. So Chapter 4 challenged you and your team to improve the working environment and your work practices so as to reduce the causes and effects of stress on you and your colleagues.

The methods which you have found to control stress at work need to become integral to your working life. One of the best ways to ensure this is through education or 'life-long learning'. So what better way than to focus on minimising stress through your personal development plan? Hopefully the worked example that we included in Chapter 5 will have given you all sorts of ideas of how you can draw up your own personal development plan.

You need to think about your situation as widely as possible, if you are to minimise stress from work effectively. If you do not anticipate and react to all of the factors that produce stress at work for you, and those that will hinder your applying your action plan, then your good intentions may come to nothing. That is why we introduced you to the 'log-frame' approach in this chapter. You should be thinking out what assumptions you are making when drawing up your action plan, and what factors will enhance your chances of carrying your action plan through and sustaining changes over time. Have you started to think of the problems that are likely to occur and foul up your plans, sending your stress levels sky high? Does your log frame anticipate these issues? Or do you need to discuss your plans now with someone else who may be able to point out your blind spots?

We hope that we have strengthened your resolve to actively control stress that arises from your work and guided you to help yourself and others in your practice, directorate or trust – to beat stress at work in the NHS.

References

1   Pattani S, Constantinovici N and Williams S (2001) Who retires early from the NHS because of ill health and what does it cost? A national cross-sectional study. *BMJ*. **322**: 208–9.

2   The National Association of Primary Care (2001) *Medical and Nursing Workforce Survey*. National Association of Primary Care, London.

3   Buchan J (2002) Global nursing shortages. *BMJ*. **324**: 751–2.

4   Williams S, Michie S and Pattani S (1998) *Improving the Health of the NHS Workforce*. Nuffield Trust, London.

5   Chambers R (1999) *Survival Skills for GPs*. Radcliffe Medical Press, Oxford.

6   Royal College of Physicians (2001) *Survey of Morale in Physician Workforce*. Third annual survey. Royal College of Physicians, London.

7   Ramirez A, Graham J, Richards M *et al.* (1996) Mental health of hospital consultants: the effects of stress and satisfaction at work. *Lancet*. **347**: 724–8.

8   Sibbald B, Enzer I, Cooper C *et al.* (2000) GP job satisfaction in 1987, 1990 and 1998: lessons for the future? *Fam Pract*. **17**: 364–71.

9   Calnan M, Wainwright D, Forsythe M *et al.* (2000) *Health and Related Behaviour Within General Practice in South Thames*. Centre for Health Services Studies, University of Kent, Canterbury.

10 Jones J, Hodgson J, Clegg T *et al.* (1998) *Self-reported Work-related Illness in 1995: results from a household survey*. Health and Safety Executive, Sudbury.

11 Cooper CL, Cooper RD and Eaker LH (1988) *Living with Stress*. Penguin, Harmondsworth.

12 Mechanic D (2001) How should hamsters run? Some observations about sufficient patient time in primary care. *BMJ*. **323**: 266–8.

13 Howe W (1999) Stress. In: SS Sadhra and KG Rampal (eds) *Occupational Health: risk assessment and management*. Blackwell Science, Oxford.

14 Borrill C and Haynes C (1999) Health service managers. In: J Firth-Cozens and R Payne (eds) *Stress in Health Professionals: psychological and organisational causes and interventions*. John Wiley & Sons, Chichester.

15 Cox T (1993) *Stress Research and Stress Management: putting theory to work*. HSE Contract Research Report No 61/1993. University of Nottingham, Nottingham.

16   Health and Safety Executive (2001) *Tackling Work-Related Stress: a manager's guide to improving and maintaining employee health and well-being.* Health and Safety Executive, Sudbury.

17   Department of Health (1999) *National Service Framework for Mental Health.* Department of Health, London.

18   North Staffordshire Health Authority (2001) *Promoting Wellbeing in North Staffordshire 2002–2005.* North Staffordshire Health Authority, Stoke-on-Trent.

19   Richards C (1989) *The Health of Doctors.* King's Fund, London.

20   General Practitioners Committee (2001) *National Survey of GP Opinion.* British Medical Association, London.

21   Borrill C and Haynes C (2000) Stressed to kill. *Health Serv J.* **10 February**: 24–5.

22   Sibbald B and Young R (2000) Job stress and mental health of GPs. *Br J Gen Pract.* **50**: 1007–8.

23   Cox T, Griffiths A, Barlowe C *et al.* (2000) *Organisational Interventions for Work Stress. A risk management approach.* Health and Safety Executive, Norwich.

24   Appleton K, House A and Dowell A (1998) A survey of job satisfaction, source of stress and psychological symptoms among GPs in Leeds. *Br J Gen Pract.* **48**: 1059–63.

25   Chambers R and Davies M (1999) *What Stress in Primary Care!* Royal College of General Practitioners, London.

26   Rosengren A, Orth-Gomer K, Wedel H *et al.* (1993) Stressful life events, social support and mortality in men born in 1933. *BMJ.* **307**: 1102–5.

27   Stahl SM and Hauger RL (1994) Stress: an overview of the literature with emphasis on job-related strain and intervention. *Adv Ther.* **11**: 110–19.

28   Scottish General Practitioners' Committee (2001) *The Reality Behind the Rhetoric.* Scottish General Practitioners' Committee, Edinburgh.

29   Ramirez A, Graham J, Richards M *et al.* (1995) Burnout and psychiatric disorder among cancer clinicians. *Br J Cancer.* **71**: 1263–9.

30   Goldman L and Lewis J (2001) The price of happiness for junior medical staff. *Employ Doctors Dentists.* **37**: 5.

31   Firth-Cozens J and Payne R (eds) (1999) *Stress in Health Professionals.* John Wiley and Sons, Chichester.

32   Chambers R, Boath E and Wakley G (2001) *Mental Health Matters in Primary Care.* Radcliffe Medical Press, Oxford.

33   Ernst E and Kanji N (2000) Autogenic training for stress and anxiety: a systematic review. *Compl Ther Med J.* **8**: 106–10.

34   Saunders T, Driskell JE, Johnston JH *et al.* (1996) The effect of stress inoculation training on anxiety and performance. *J Occup Health Psychol.* **April** 1(2): 170–86.

35   Sims J (1997) The evaluation of stress management strategies in general practice: an evidence-led approach. *Br J Gen Pract.* **47**: 577–82.

36   Meichenbaum D (1985) *Stress Inoculation Training*. Pergamon Press, New York.

37   Meichenbaum D (1993) Stress inoculation training: a twenty-year update. In: R Woolfolk and PM Lehrer (eds) *Principles and Practices of Stress Management*. Guilford Press, New York.

38   Wilkinson G, Moore B and Moore P (2000) *Treating People with Anxiety and Stress*. Radcliffe Medical Press, Oxford.

39   Kabat-Zinn J (1990) *Full Catastrophe Living*. Delta, New York.

40   Bishop SR (2002) What do we really know about mindfulness-based stress reduction? *Altern Ther Health Med*. **8**: 60–6.

41   Claxton G (1997) *Hare Brain, Tortoise Mind*. Fourth Estate Ltd, London.

42   Claxton G (1999) *Wise Up: the challenge of lifelong learning*. Bloomsbury Publishing, London.

43   Weatherall M (2002) Small victories that make every day a different one. *BMA News*. **30 March**: 6.

44   Neck CP and Manz CC (1992) Thought self-leadership: the influence of self-talk and mental imagery on performance. *J Organiz Behav*. **13**: 681–99.

45   Munz DC, Huelsman TJ and Craft CA (1995) A worksite stress management program: theory, application and outcomes. In: LR Murphy, JJ Hurrell, SL Sauter *et al*. (eds) *Job Stress Interventions*. American Psychological Association, Washington, DC.

46   Jones L and Stuth G (1997) The uses of mental imagery in athletics: an overview. *Appl Prev Psychol*. **6**: 101–15.

47   Ainsworth-Land V (1991) Imaging and creativity: an integrating perspective. In: J Henry (ed.) *Creative Management*. Sage, London.

48   Cooperrider DL (1990) Positive image, positive action: the affirmative basis of organising. In: S Srivastva and DL Cooperrider (eds) *Appreciative Management and Leadership*. Jossey-Bass, San Francisco, CA.

49   Wheatley WJ, Maddox EN and Anthony WP (1989) Enhancing creativity and imagination in strategic planners through the utilization of guided imagery. *Org Dev J*. **Winter**: 36–44.

50   Gelder M (1998) The scientific foundations of cognitive behaviour therapy. In: DM Clark and CG Fairburn (eds) *Science and Practice of Cognitive Behaviour Therapy*. Oxford University Press, Oxford.

51   Layden MA (1998) *Workshop on Using Visualisation with Personality Disorder*. Workshop proceedings, Richmond.

52   Brigham D (1994) *Imagery for Getting Well: clinical applications of behavioral medicine*. Norton Press, London.

53   Hammer SE (1996) The effects of guided imagery through music on state and trait anxiety. *J Music Ther*. **33**: 47–70.

54   Stephens R (1993) Imagery: a strategic intervention to empower clients. *Clin Nurse Specialist*. **7**: 170–4.

55 Black J (1996) *Mindstore for Personal Development*. Thorsons, London.

56 Goleman D (1995) *Emotional Intelligence*. Bantam, New York.

57 Graham H (1995) *Mental Imagery in Health Care*. Chapman and Hall, London.

58 Shone R (1984) *Creative Visualization*. Thorsons, New York.

59 Mills H (1996) *The Mental Edge*. Simon and Schuster, East Roseville, Australia.

60 Maw J and Maw J (1995) Imagery, self-esteem and laughter. *Occu Health*. **February**: 55–7.

61 Dainow S (1998) *Working and Surviving in Organisations*. John Wiley and Sons, Chichester.

62 Stephens R (1993) Imagery: a strategic intervention to empower clients. *Clin Nurse Specialist*. **7**: 170–4.

63 Vines SW (1994) Relaxation with guided imagery: effects on employees' psychological distress and health-seeking behaviours. *Am Assoc Occup Health Nurs J*. **42**: 206–13.

64 Dossey B (1991) Awakening the Inner Healer. *Am J Nurs*. **August**: 31–4.

65 Tyssen R, Vaglum P, Gronvold N *et al.* (2000) The impact of job stress and working conditions on mental health problems among junior house officers. A nationwide Norwegian prospective cohort study. *Med Educ*. **34**: 374–84.

66 Hawkins P and Shohet R (1989) *Supervision in the Helping Professions*. Open University Press, Milton Keynes.

67 Maddocks M (2000) Working wounded. *Health Serv J*. **13 January**: 26–7.

68 Chambers R, Mohanna K and Field S (2000) *Opportunities and Options in Medical Careers*. Radcliffe Medical Press, Oxford.

69 Schein E (1990) *Career Anchors: discovering your real needs*. Pfeiffer and Co., Oxford.

70 Carlisle D (2002) Family-friendly route way forward for trainee GPs. *BMA News*. **23 March**: 8.

71 Dumelow C, Littlejohns P and Griffiths S (2000) The inter-relationship between a medical career and family life for hospital consultants: an interview survey. *BMJ*. **320**: 1437–40.

72 Department of Health (2002) *Statistics for General Medical Practitioners in England: 1991–2001*. Department of Health, London.

73 Kivimaki M, Sutinen R, Elovainio M *et al.* (2001) Sickness absence in hospital physicians: 2-year follow-up study on determinants. *Occup Environ Med*. **58**: 361–6.

74 Thompson W, Cupples M, Sibbett C *et al.* (2001) Challenge of culture, conscience and contract to general practitioners' care of their own health: qualitative study. *BMJ*. **323**: 728–31.

75 Bandura A (1995) *Self-Efficacy in Changing Societies*. Cambridge University Press, Cambridge.

76   Parker S and Williams H (2001) *Effective Teamworking: reducing the psychosocial risks.* Health and Safety Executive, Norwich.

77   Myerson S (1992) Problems in UK general practice since the new contract [1990] and general practitioners' strategies for dealing with them. *Med Sci Res.* **20**: 461–3.

78   Salovey P and Mayer JD (1990) Emotional intelligence. *Imagination Cogn Pers.* **9**: 185–211.

79   Mayer JD and Salovey P (1993) The intelligence of emotional intelligence. *Intelligence.* **17**: 433–42.

80   Hart E and Fletcher J (1999) Learning how to change: a selective analysis of literature and experience of how teams learn and organisations change. *J Interprof Care.* **13**: 53–63.

81   Firth-Cozens J (1998) Elements that encourage good teamworking. *Qual Health Care.* **7 (Supplement)**: 1–24.

82   Miller C, Ross N and Freeman M (1999) *Shared Learning and Clinical Teamwork: new directions in education and multiprofessional practice.* English National Board for Nursing, Midwifery and Health Visiting, University of Brighton, Brighton.

83   West M and Wallace M (1991) Innovation in health care teams. *Eur J Soc Psychol.* **21**: 303–15.

84   Elwyn G and Smail J (1999) *Integrated Teams in Primary Care.* Radcliffe Medical Press, Oxford.

85   Suresh K (2002) Tips on … leading your team. *BMJ Careers.* **324**: 103.

86   Woodham A (1995) *Beating Stress at Work.* Health Education Authority, London.

87   Chambers R, George V, McNeill A *et al.* (1998) Health at work in the general practice. *Br J Gen Pract* **48**: 1501–4.

88   Lilley R (1999) *Making Sense of Clinical Governance.* Radcliffe Medical Press, Oxford.

89   Department of Health (1998) *A First-Class Service: quality in the new NHS.* Health Service Circular HSC (98)113. Department of Health, London.

90   Chambers R and Wakley G (2000) *Making Clinical Governance Work for You.* Radcliffe Medical Press, Oxford.

91   Wakley G, Chambers R and Field S (2000) *Continuing Professional Development in Primary Care: making it happen.* Radcliffe Medical Press, Oxford.

92   Cohen S, Kamarck T and Mermelstein R (1983) Perceived Stress Scale. A global measure of perceived stress. *J Health Soc Behav.* **24**: 385–96.

93   Moos RH (1994) *Work Environment Scale: a social climate scale. Work environment manual.* Consulting Psychologists Press, Palo Alto, CA.

94   Coleman G (1987) Logical framework approach to the monitoring and evaluation of agricultural and rural development projects. *Project Appraisal.* **2**: 251–9.

95   Centre for Rural Development and Training (2000) *A Guide for Developing a Logical Framework.* University of Wolverhampton, Wolverhampton.

96   Jacobs B (2001) *Logical Framework and Performance Management.* North Staffordshire Health Action Zone, Stoke-on-Trent.

97   Spender A and Chambers R (2001) *Logical Framework Plan for Teenwise Project.* Staffordshire University, Stoke-on-Trent (unpublished). Project report to the Department of Health.

Useful resources for the management of stress

Further reading

Relating to employers' responsibilities and workplaces

- Cartwright S and Cooper C (1997) *Managing Workplace Stress*. Sage, London.
- Cooper C and Cartwright S (1996) *Mental Health and Stress in the Workplace: a guide for employers*. HMSO, London.
- Doherty N and Tyson S (1998) *Mental Wellbeing in the Workplace. A resource pack for management training and development*. HMSO, Norwich.
- Floyd M, Povall M and Watson G (eds) (1994) Mental health at work. In: *Disability and Rehabilitation. Series 5*. Jessica Kingsley, London.
- Industrial Society (1995) Stress management. In: *Managing Best Practice*. Industrial Society, London.
- Kogan H (ed.) (1997) *The Corporate Healthcare Handbook*. Kogan Page, London.

Health at Work in the NHS publications (previously published by the Health Education Authority, now the Health Development Agency)

- Health at Work in the NHS (1996) *NHS Staff Needs Assessment: a practice guide*. Health Education Authority, London.
- Health at Work in the NHS (1996) *Organisational Stress: planning and implementing a programme to address organisational stress in the NHS*. Health Education Authority, London.
- Health at Work in the NHS (1997) *Working for Your Health: a survey of NHS trust staff*. Health Education Authority, London.
- Health at Work in the NHS (1997) *Risk Assessment at Work: practical examples in the NHS*. Health Education Authority, London.
- Health at Work in the NHS (1997) *GP Investigatory Study*. Health Education Authority, London.
- Health at Work in the NHS (1998) *NE Essex Mental Health Trust Organisational Stress Pilot: a case study*. Health Education Authority, London.

- Health at Work in the NHS (1998) *Survey of General Practices: health at work in primary care research study.* Health Education Authority, London.
- Health at Work in the NHS (1998) *General Practice Resources Directory: for promoting health at work.* Health Education Authority, London.
- Health at Work in the NHS (1998) *Health and Safety in General Practice: a guide to risk assessment for GPs and practice managers.* Health Education Authority, London.
- Health at Work in the NHS (1999) *Listening for Health: a guide to effective workplace counselling.* Health Education Authority, London.
- Health at Work in the NHS (1999) *Building Blocks for a Healthier Workplace: health needs assessment guidance.* Health Education Authority, London.
- Health at Work in the NHS (1999) *Work-Related Stress Initiatives Set 2: three case studies.* Health Education Authority, London.
- Health at Work in the NHS (2000) *Work-Related Stress Initiatives Set 3: three case studies.* Health Education Authority, London.
- Health at Work in the NHS (2001) *New Primary Care Premises: design to support workplace health.* Health Development Agency, London.
- Health at Work in the NHS (2001) *Workplace Health in Small Practices: issues for GPs and their staff.* Health Development Agency, London.
- Health at Work in the NHS (2001) *Violence and Aggression in General Practice: guidance on assessment and management.* Health Development Agency, London.
- Health at Work in the NHS (2001) *Workplace Health is Good Practice: framework for action in primary care.* Health Development Agency, London.
- Health at Work in the NHS (2001) *Framework for Action: guidance for primary care trusts.* Health Development Agency, London.
- Health at Work in the NHS (2001) *Framework for Action: health at work in the NHS.* Health Development Agency, London.

Individuals' management of own stress

- Atkinson S (1993) *Climbing Out of Depression: a practical guide for sufferers.* Lion Publishing, Oxford.
- Clarke D (1994) *How to Manage Stress.* National Extension College, London.
- Cooper CL (2000) *Theories of Organisational Stress.* Oxford University Press, Oxford.
- Cooper CL and Palmer S (2000) *Conquer Your Stress.* Chartered Institute of Personnel and Development, London.
- Cozens J (1991) *OK2 Talk Feelings.* BBC Books, London.
- Davies P (1996) *Personal Power: how to become more assertive and successful at work.* Piatkus, London.

- Denny R (1997) *Succeed for Yourself: unlock your potential for success and happiness.* Kogan Page, London.
- Gillett R (1991) *Overcoming Depression: a practical self-help guide to prevention and treatment.* Dorling Kindersley, London.
- Goleman D (1996) *Emotional Intelligence.* Bloomsbury Publishing, London.
- Harris TA (1973) *I'm OK, You're OK.* Pan Books, London.
- Jackson G, Kassianos G, Koppel S *et al.* (2000) Depression: a guide to its recognition and management in general practice. *Guidelines.* **11**: 1171–4.
- Jeffers S (1987) *Feel the Fear and Do It Anyway.* Rider, London.
- Milligan S and Clare A (1993) *Depression and How to Survive It.* Arrow, London.
- Rowe D (1996) *Depression: the way out of your prison.* Routledge, London.
- Schwartz AL and Dennis E (1998) Developing human potential workshops with staff groups focusing on 'positive images – positive steps'. *Clin Psychol Forum.* **117**: 18–19.
- Skynner R and Cleese J (1994) *Families and How to Survive Them.* Mandarin, London.
- Weekes C (1981) *Self-Help for Your Nerves.* Harper Collins, London.
- Weekes C (1983) *Peace from Nervous Suffering.* Bantam Books, London.
- Wilkinson G, Moore B and Moore P (2000) *Treating People with Depression. A practical guide for primary care.* Radcliffe Medical Press, Oxford.
- Wilkinson G, Moore B and Moore P (2000) *Treating People with Anxiety and Stress. A practical guide for primary care.* Radcliffe Medical Press, Oxford.

Audio cassettes relating to stress management

Talking Life, PO Box 1, Wirral CH47 7DD
Tel: 0151 632 0662 Fax: 0151 632 1206
Website: www.talkinglife.co.uk

You can order audio cassettes on *Coping with Stress at Work, Coping with Depression, Stress Kit, Feeling Good, Relaxation Kit, Anxiety/Depression Option Pack* and many others, such as *Stress Multi Packs* and Training Packs (*Depression Skills Pack, Stress Management Packs, Anxiety and Depression Packs*).

Organisations that provide help with workplace approaches to stress

Arcadia Alive Ltd, Consultancy, Training and Development
Parkfield Centre, Park Street, Stafford ST17 4AL
Tel: 01785 223253
Website: www.arcadiaalive.com

Confederation of British Industry (CBI), Scotland
16 Robertson Street, Glasgow G2 8DS
Tel: 0141 222 2184

Employment Medical Advisory Service (EMAS) Health and Safety Executive
EMAS Health and Safety Executive has offices throughout the country that are staffed by doctors and nurses with occupational health qualifications. EMAS provides free advice and support to employers and employees with regard to work-related medical problems, including mental health problems.
Tel: 01342 334200

Entec UK Limited
Doherty Innovation Centre, Pentlands Science Park, Bush Loane, Penicuik, Midlothian EH26 0PZ
Tel: 0131 445 6112

Health and Safety Executive
Rose Court, 2 Southwark Bridge, London SE1 9HS
Tel: 0207 717 6000 Fax: 0207 717 6890/6086
Belford House, 59 Belford Road, Edinburgh EH8 9SU
InfoLine Tel: 0541 545500

Health Development Agency (HDA)
The HDA offers a range of expertise on mental health and well-being. Information on the NHS, small and medium-sized business enterprises, and the Health at Work resources that were developed in that project's lifetime can be obtained by writing to:
Workplace Health, Health Development Agency, Trevelyan House, 30 Great Peter Street, London SW1P 2HW
Tel: 0207 413 1873

International Stress Management Association UK
The International Stress Management Association UK is a registered charity that aims to promote sound knowledge and best practice in the prevention

147

and reduction of human stress. It sets professional standards for the benefit of individuals and organisations using the services of its members.
PO Box 348, Waltham Cross EN8 8ZL
Tel: 07000 780430
Website: www.isma.org.uk

Scottish Trades Union Congress (STUC)
333 Woodlands Road, Glasgow G3 6NG
Tel: 0141 337 8100

Trades Union Congress
Congress House, Great Russell Street, London WC1B 3LS
Tel: 0207 636 4030 Fax: 0207 636 0632
Website: www.tuc.org.uk

National and voluntary organisations

Action on Addiction
1st Floor, Park Place, 12 Lawn Lane, London SW8 1UD
Tel: 0207 793 1011
Website: www.aona.co.uk

Advisory Council on Alcohol and Drug Education
1 Hulme Place, The Crescent, Salford, Manchester M5 4QA
Tel: 0161 745 8925
Website: www.tacade.com

African–Caribbean Mental Health Association
49 Effra Road, Suite 37, London SW2 1BZ
Tel: 0207 737 3603

Alcohol Advisory Service
309 Grays Inn Road, London WC1X 8QF
Tel: 0207 530 5900

Alcohol Concern
Alcohol Concern is the national agency on alcohol misuse. It supplies information on alcoholism and details of local services.
Waterbridge House, 32–36 Loman Street, London SE1 0EE
Tel: 0207 928 7377
Helpline: 0800 917 8282 (24 hours)
Website: www.alcoholconcern.org.uk

Alcoholics Anonymous
Alcoholics Anonymous is a fellowship of people who share their experiences in order to help others to recover from alcoholism and remain sober.
PO Box 1, Stonebow House, Stonebow, York YO1 7NJ
Tel: 01904 644026 (Office Mon–Thurs 9am–5pm, Fri 9am–4.30pm)
Helpline: 0845 769 7555
London helpline: 0207 833 0022 (10am–10pm daily)
Website: www.alcoholics-anonymous.org.uk

British Association for Counselling (BACS)
BACS provides information and advice on counselling and counsellors in the UK.
1 Regent Place, Rugby, Warwickshire CV21 2PJ
Tel: 01788 578328 (24-hour information line)
Website: www.bac.co.uk

British Association of Psychotherapists
37 Mapesbury Road, London NW2 4HJ
Tel: 0208 452 9823

British Association for Sexual and Marital Therapy
PO Box 62, Sheffield, South Yorkshire S10 3TL

British Medical Association (BMA)
BMA House, Tavistock Square, London WC1H 9JP
Tel (Head Office): 0207 387 4499 Email: enquiries@bma.org.uk
Website (news): www.bma.org.uk

BMA Counselling Service
This telephone advice line is for members and their families, and it offers a 24-hour service.
Tel: 08459 200169

Carers National Association
20–25 Glass House Yard, London EC1A 4JT
Tel: 0207 490 8818
Website: www.carersonline.org.uk

Chronic Illness Matching Scheme
This scheme is open to all doctors and medical students in the UK.
Website: www.bma.org.uk/public/chill.nsf

Compassionate Friends
53 North Street, Bristol BS3 1EN
Tel: 0117 966 5202 Helpline: 0117 953 9639

Counselling in Primary Care Trust
First Floor, Majestic House, High Street, Staines TW18 4DG
Tel: 01784 441782 Fax: 01784 442601
Website: www.cpct.co.uk

CRUSE Bereavement Care
CRUSE is a national voluntary organisation that offers bereavement counselling and advice. It has branches in all areas. Contact via the local telephone directory or:
Tel: 0208 940 4818 Helpline: 0208 332 7227 (9.30am–5pm Mon–Fri).

Depression Alliance
The Depression Alliance runs a network of self-help groups, and also provides information, support and advice for those who suffer from depression, as well as for their carers.
35 Westminster Bridge Road, London SE1 7JB
Tel: 0207 633 0557
Website: www.depressionalliance.org

Depressives Anonymous
This organisation is run as a source of support for sufferers. It can put enquirers in contact with local groups.
36 Chestnut Avenue, Beverley, East Yorkshire HU17 9QU
Tel: 01482 860619

The Doctor–Patient Partnership
This organisation provides useful references, websites, addresses, national helplines and guidelines for the management of stress.
Tel: 0207 383 6803 Email: dpp@bma.org.uk
Website: www.dpp.org.uk

Doctors' Support Network
This organisation offers support to doctors with mental illness.
Tel: 0707 122 3372
Email: lizzie.miller@talk21.com

Drinkline
First Floor Cavern Court, 8 Matthew Street, Liverpool L2 6RE
Helpline: 0800 917 8282 Dial and Listen: 0500 801802
Website: www.wrecked.co.uk

Drugaid
16 Clyve Street, Caerphilly CF83 1GE
Tel: 0292 088 1000

DrugScope
32–36 Loman Street, London SE1 0EE
Tel: 0207 928 1211
Website: www.drugscope.org.uk

Eating Disorders Association
First Floor, Wensum House, 103 Prince of Wales Road, Norwich NR1 1DW
Tel: 01603 619090 Helpline: 01603 621414

Enable
Sixth Floor, 7 Buchanan Street, Glasgow G1 3HL
Tel: 0141 226 4541

Faculty of Occupational Medicine of the Royal College of Physicians
6 St Andrews Place, Regent's Park, London NW1 4LB
Tel: 0207 317 5890
Website: www.facoccmed.ac.uk

Fellowship of Depressives Anonymous (FDA)
Box FDA, Self-Help Nottingham, Ormiston House, 32–36 Pelham Street, Nottingham NG1 2EG
Information line: 01702 433838

Gamblers Anonymous
PO Box 88, London SW10 0EU
Helpline: 0207 384 3040 (24 hours)

Health Education Board for Scotland (HEBS)
Woodburn House, Canaan Lane, Edinburgh EH10 4SG
Tel: 0131 536 5500 Fax: 0131 536 5501
Email: library.enquiries@hebs.scot.nhs.uk
Website: www.hebs.scot.nhs.uk

International Stress Management Association
PO Box 348, Waltham Cross, London EN8 8ZL
Tel: 07000 780430
Website: www.isma.org.uk

Mental Health Foundation
This charity provides information both for the general public and for health and social care professionals.
20/21 Cornwall Terrace, London NW1 4QL
Tel: 0207 535 7400

MIND (National Association for Mental Health)
MIND offers a range of day-care and other services, and provides information and publications on mental health issues and services. It makes information available about most matters concerned with mental health. MIND is open to users, carers, family and friends, researchers, students, service providers and the public, and it can direct enquirers to local support groups. Listed in the local telephone directory, or contact via:
Granta House, 15–19 Broadway, London E15 4BQ
Tel: 08457 660163 National helpline: 0345 660163
Website: www.mind.org.uk

National Counselling Service for Sick Doctors
This is an independent advisory service for doctors in the UK.
Tel: 0870 241 0535
Website: www.ncssd.org.uk

National Phobics Society
Zion Community Resource Centre, 339 Stretford Road, Hulme, Manchester M15 4ZY
Tel: 0870 7700 456
Website: www.phobics-society.org.uk

NHS Careers
Website: www.nhscareers.nhs.uk

No Panic
93 Brands Farm Way, Telford, Shropshire TF3 2JQ
Tel: 01952 590005 Helpline: 0808 808 0545 (10am–10pm)
Website: www.no-panic.co.uk

Relate
Relate has branches throughout the UK, providing couple counselling for relationship breakdown.
Herbert Gray College, Little Church Street, Rugby, Warwickshire CV21 3AP
Tel: 01788 573241
Website: www.relate.org.uk

Samaritans
The Samaritans is a UK telephone helpline that provides someone to talk to in confidence 24 hours a day, every day of the year. The organisation offers support to those in distress who feel suicidal or despairing and need someone to talk to. The number of the local branch can be found in the telephone directory or obtained from the telephone operator.
46 Marshall Street, London W1V 1LR
Tel: 01753 532713 National helpline: 08457 909090
Website: www.samaritans.org.uk

SANE
SANE provides information and support for carers, sufferers and friends.
First Floor, Cityside House, 40 Adler Street, London E1 1EE
Tel: 0207 375 1002 National helpline: 0845 767 8000
Website: www.sane.org.uk

Scottish Association for Mental Health
Cumbrae House, 15 Carlton House, Glasgow G5 9JP
Tel: 0141 568 7000

Seasonal Affective Disorders Association
PO Box 989, Steyning BN44 3HG
Website: www.sada.org.uk

Sick Doctors Trust
This organisation offers doctors help with regard to alcohol and drug addiction.
Tel: 01252 345163

Sleep Council
High Corn Mill, Chapel Hill, Skipton BD23 1NL
Tel: 01756 791089
Website: www.sleepcouncil.org.uk

Someone To Talk To
Someone To Talk To offers free advice and support, and confidential counselling, by qualified therapists and counsellors on issues such as relationship difficulties and breakdown, stress, depression, anxiety and other mental health worries via email, telephone and post.
Someone To Talk To, PO Box 245, St Albans AL3 5YW
Tel: 01727 868813 Fax: 01727 868813
Email: Advice@someonetotalkto.co.uk
Website: www.someonetotalkto.co.uk

Stressbusting
Website: www.stressbusting.co.uk

Stresswatch Scotland
The Barn, 42 Barnweil Road, Kilmarnock KA1 4JE
Tel: 01563 574144 Helpline: 01563 528910

Turning Point
Turning Point provides help with and advice on problems with alcohol, drugs, mental health and learning disabilities.
101 Backchurch Lane, London E1 1LU
Tel: 0207 702 2300
Website: www.turning-point.co.uk

Index